"The emergence of modern Pentecostalism at Azuza Street promised an ecumenism of the church that cut across the color line but which fulfillment has been derailed in North America at least by the history of racism in this country. The emergence of a 'Pentecostal orthodoxy' over the last fifty years—catalyzed vigorously by the Chicago Call (to evangelicals in 1977), the paleo-orthodox movement (Thomas Oden), ancient-future Christianity (Robert Webber), and other initiatives—promises an even more authentically charismatic and ever more radically renewed ecumenism of the Spirit that binds together not just those from every nation under heaven but also churches across the last two millennia of African, Orthodox, Catholic, and Reformation/Anglican traditions! Come Holy Spirit—be poured out again on all peoples, languages, and cultures/ethnicities for the twenty-first-century church's witness!"

Amos Yong, professor of theology and mission at Fuller Seminary

"*Pentecostal Orthodoxy* opens a new chapter in ecumenism, Pentecostalism, and world Christianity. The breadth and depth of its scholarship is extraordinary. With integrity and passion, Emilio Alvarez has demonstrated that an authentic recovery of the Great Tradition opens up the renewing power of the Spirit for all streams of Christian faith today."

Dale T. Irvin, professor of world Christianity at New School of Biblical Theology and adjunct in theology and religious studies at Georgetown University

"Let's be honest, when most people think of Pentecostals, orthodoxy is not the first thing that comes to mind. For many of us, these words represent a paradox. However, as Bishop Emilio Alvarez successfully demonstrates, orthodoxy and Pentecostalism do belong together. He documents a movement where the Spirit is leading thousands of Pentecostals to defy this false dichotomy and rediscover the Great Tradition for today. Alvarez is on the forefront of this movement and has written an essential manifesto for the church, calling for Pentecostals to embrace Christian orthodoxy. More than that, he paints a hopeful picture of the future of the church as one that is historically rooted and modern; orthodox and gracious; unified and diverse; sacramental and open to the Spirit. This book is a major resource for anyone wanting to know about one of the most exciting things that the Spirit is doing in the church today."

Winfield Bevins, author of *Liturgical Mission: The Work of the People for the Sake of the World*

"During these times when 'truth is on a scaffold and wrong is on the throne,' Bishop Alvarez becomes the voice in this wilderness. He crowbars the mind with terminology such as Pentecostal orthodoxy, ecumenism of the Spirit, and surely, the recovery of the Great Tradition. This work is nothing short of a revival road map. Dr. Alvarez, who once preached revivals in local churches, now pens revivals with the same passion necessary for the salvation of 'the saved.' Here, like Jacob, the bishop re-digs old wells. Hallelujah!"

Johnny Ray Youngblood, ▭▭▭h Baptist Church in Brooklyn, New York

"'Sankofa' teaches that we r ▭▭▭ ad. That is, we should reach back and gather the best ▭▭▭ ieve our full potential as we go forward. In *Pentecost* ▭▭▭ rican Latino Pentecostals to proudly stand on the sh ▭▭▭ nend this edition to be both read and studied by those ▭▭▭ on within the Holiness Pentecostal evolution of the church. Let us consider g▭▭▭ ts of the Great Tradition so as to better move forward to achieve a spiritually empowered future of the Lord's church."

David M. Copeland, chairman of the board of The Joint College of African American Pentecostal Bishops

"In *Pentecostal Orthodoxy*, Emilio Alvarez surprises the reader with how the Great Tradition has been engaged by the African Orthodox Church and the Church of God in Christ. Then he creatively instructs us on the value of being taught by the Great Tradition itself. This stellar book models a generative form of ecumenical engagement."

David D. Daniels, Henry Winters Luce Professor of World Christianity at McCormick
Theological Seminary

"The vital and often Pentecostal faith of immigrant churches holds much promise for the future renewal of the US church. Such hope, however, may become sabotaged by the ticking time bomb of incomplete theology. Alvarez's framework of Pentecostal orthodoxy offers a healthy path forward."

Robert Chao Romero, associate professor in the Departments of Chicana/o Studies and Asian
American Studies at the University of California at Los Angeles, author of *Brown Church*

"*Pentecostal Orthodoxy* is the first scholarly book of its kind and a much-needed addition to the growing canon of *Pentecostal studies*. With conviction and accessibility, Pentecostal Orthodoxy wrestles with what it means to love Christ and the church. Throughout, Bishop Alvarez proves that he is not only a premier intellectual thought leader of Pentecostal orthodoxy but also a spiritual guide. The text, therefore, is his formal invitation for all of us to sit, think, and pray with him about what it would mean if the church were truly one, holy, and catholic."

Dara Coleby Delgado, assistant professor of religious studies and Black studies at
Allegheny College

"The Pentecostal movement needs more works like this. Alvarez adroitly navigates the thorny terrain in which contemporary Black Pentecostalism finds itself as it moves away from fundamentalist evangelical thinking 'toward more liturgical, sacramental, and creedal forms of Christianity.' Alvarez presents contemporary faith leaders with important questions for the future: Are Christianity and orthodoxy commensurate, in view of the persistence of categorical racism? Is orthodoxy a form of theological reasoning that can liberate Black Pentecostals from deep-seated racism that persists in Western Christian culture? And what are the ramifications of Alvarez's claims for organizations that adhere to an episcopal polity like the Joint College of African American Pentecostal Bishops? You will have to purchase your own copy to find out. I recommend this book for pastors and scholars, church leaders and lay people."

Donald Hilliard Jr., senior pastor of Cathedral International, Perth Amboy, New Jersey

"*Pentecostal Orthodoxy* is a pioneering and provocative work of scholarship and renewing spirituality! As a pioneering work it breaks new ground by mapping and introducing the emerging Spirit-led growth of the 'ecumenism of the Spirit' among the Pentecostal church and beyond—one that is richly sourced by Eastern Orthodoxy. As a provocative work it challenges Pentecostals to embrace orthodoxy as a Spirit-led grassroots movement that coheres well with Pentecostal spirituality. This Pentecostal orthodoxy is one that seeks to be informed, formed, and transformed by the Great Tradition, with its newly found profundity in the liturgical and sacramental. This book should be required reading for all persons (Pentecostal or not) interested in the life and mission of the one church."

Eldin Villafañe, distinguished senior professor emeritus of Christian social ethics at Gordon
Conwell Theological Seminary

Pentecostal Orthodoxy

Toward an Ecumenism
of the Spirit

Emilio Alvarez

Foreword by John Behr

ivp
Academic
An imprint of InterVarsity Press
Downers Grove, Illinois

2 81.9

InterVarsity Press
P.O. Box 1400 | Downers Grove, IL 60515-1426
ivpress.com | email@ivpress.com

©2022 by Emilio Alvarez

All rights reserved. No part of this book may be reproduced in any form without written permission from InterVarsity Press.

InterVarsity Press® is the publishing division of InterVarsity Christian Fellowship/USA®. For more information, visit intervarsity.org.

Scripture taken from the New King James Version®. Copyright © 1982 by Thomas Nelson. Used by permission. All rights reserved.

The publisher cannot verify the accuracy or functionality of website URLs used in this book beyond the date of publication.

Cover design and image composite: David Fassett
Interior design: Daniel van Loon

ISBN 978-1-5140-0090-8 (print) | ISBN 978-1-5140-0091-5 (digital)

Printed in the United States of America ∞

Library of Congress Cataloging-in-Publication Data
A catalog record for this book is available from the Library of Congress.

28 27 26 25 24 23 22 | 8 7 6 5 4 3 2 1

This book is dedicated to my old man,

Mi Viejo Emilio Alvarez Sr.

Dad,

Words will never be able to describe what you mean to me. Thank you for loving me without reservation and for walking with me through the most difficult of moments. This book is both an embodiment as well as an extension of your passion and zeal for God and his church, which I have witnessed all my life. I am honored not only to carry your legacy but to do so carrying your name ... Emilio.

Love you, Viejo!

CONTENTS

FOREWORD

JOHN BEHR

"BEHOLD, I MAKE ALL THINGS NEW," says the unveiled Christ (Rev 21:5). Renewal is at the heart of Christianity, not only the renewal of those who hear and receive the gospel but also the renewal of gospel preaching and, indeed, the church, the bride of Christ. In a series of visions, Hermas sees the church as an old woman, the first of creation, for whose sake the world was made, gradually becoming younger until she becomes "a virgin, adorned as if coming from a bridal chamber."[1] Probably alluding to this, Saint Irenaeus of Lyons speaks of the preaching of the church, and the church itself, as "renewing its [and her] youth."[2] If the church is the bride of Christ, the wedding feast is nevertheless not until the final end: the bridegroom has been revealed, and the bride is now being prepared by building up the fullness of humanity, the witness of the martyrs for the faith, so that the wedding can be consummated. The preparation of the bride is the work of Christ himself (cf. Eph 5:25-27) and is overseen by that "other counsellor," the Spirit, reminding us of all that Christ taught (Jn 14:16, 26). And so, as Saint Irenaeus also put it in the same passage: "Where the Church is, there is the Spirit of God; and where the Spirit of God is, there is the Church and all grace; and 'the Spirit is truth.'" The truth of the church, her identity and being, is eschatological.

In this time in between—between the definitive, once-for-all work of Christ and its eschatological consummation—it is not surprising that the history of Christianity is punctuated by renewals. While the language of

---

[1] "The Shepherd of Hermas," in *The Apostolic Fathers: Volume II*, ed. and trans. Kirsopp Lake, Loeb Classical Library (Cambridge, MA: Harvard University Press, 1976), 4.2.1.

[2] Irenaeus of Lyons, *Against the Heresies*, trans. Dominic J. Unger, rev. Irenaeus M. C. Steenberg, ACW 64 (New York: Newman Press, 2012), 3.24.1; 1 John 5:6.

renewal might seem to be more aligned with forms of Protestant Christianity, especially the various revival movements, it should be borne in mind that both Eastern Orthodoxy and Roman Catholicism underwent dramatic forms of renewal in the twentieth century. In both cases it involved a return to the Fathers and was also accompanied by significant liturgical and spiritual renewals. In the case of the former, the theology of the previous generations was memorably described by Father Georges Florovsky as having been a "pseudomorphosis" of authentic Orthodox theology, a "Western captivity" in which Eastern Orthodox theology had been alienated but from which it could be liberated (by émigrés in the West) through a return to the Fathers, a return also undertaken in the *resourcement* movement of theology in Roman Catholicism. The liturgical renewal of both were equally though differently profound: the resumption of the practice of frequent Communion, the reading of the prayers aloud and the adoption of the local languages for the Orthodox communities, together with a rediscovery of more ancient forms of iconography, and the revision of the Roman rite after the Second Vatican Council. And in both cases, though with roots going back several centuries, this involved the renewal of monasticism and different forms of monasticism and the propagation of, for instance, the Jesus Prayer to a wider body of believers. So profound were these developments that one can speak of Orthodoxy and Roman Catholicism as having been "born again" in the past century.[3]

These renewals should be, as I mentioned, borne in mind, for they help us understand the broader context of stirrings elsewhere. The main thesis of this present book is that something similar is underway in certain circles in Pentecostalism. That similar phenomena happened in evangelical circles over the last decades of the twentieth century is well known and surveyed here, along with a considered reflection on criteria: the Chicago Call of 1977, Thomas Oden's Paleo-Orthodoxy, the Convergence Worship Movement, and the Ancient-Future Movement, among others. What characterized all these was the desire to return to historic roots and continuity, faithfulness to the Scriptures as read and understood by the

---

[3]Thus, the title of the book by Nicholas Zernov, *The Russian Religious Renaissance of the Twentieth Century* (London: DLT, 1963).

ancient church, creedal identity, a fuller understanding of salvation, sacramental worship, and ecclesial authority and unity. Although in some cases this desire led to a "return home," as it was described by converts to Eastern Orthodoxy and Roman Catholicism. This was not uniformly the case; though, the desire for an authentic immersion into ancient Christianity continues to burn.

What, then, of Pentecostalism? Bishop Emilio Alvarez describes, often in very personal terms, the way in which some, in particular among the Afro-Latino communities, have been led to seek greater theological depths and liturgical and spiritual riches in the early church, combining their attention to ortho-pathy with orthodoxy—theological and liturgical— leading to the formation of communities such as the Union of Charismatic Orthodox Churches. Bishop Alvarez describes other attempts to recover the Great Tradition, or at least elements of it, by African American and Afro-Latino Christians in North America (in particular, The Church of God in Christ, The African Orthodox Church, and the Joint College of African American Pentecostal Bishops). He also speaks with candor and sensitivity about the way in which such attempts sometimes became a form of "mimicry" (in the sense used by Homi Bhabhi). Yet there is here, nevertheless, a serious desire and attempt to learn from the early church in matters theological, liturgical, and spiritual and also from their modern exponents, especially Eastern Orthodox (the name and influence of Father Alexander Schmemann is referred to frequently in this book).

Echoing Nathanael's question (Jn 1:46), Bishop Emilio provocatively titles his second chapter "Can Anything Orthodox Come from Pentecostalism?" This question is indeed a fascinating one, and perhaps more so with respect to the Afro-Latino Charismatic experience specifically. Is there a difference between, on the one hand, the way in which Eastern Orthodox or Roman Catholics, who have always claimed continuity or identity with the ancient church (despite periods subsequently designated a *pseudomorphosis*), experience a renewal by returning to the sources and the way in which those who have responded to the gospel proclamation in different contexts return to the same sources? Is it a return or a turn? For it is, after all, a new encounter with previously or largely unfamiliar material. Can those whose experience of Christianity has been as an oppressive White man's religion (re)turn to those ancient sources—including Egyptian, Ethiopic, Syrian, and others—and find in them more or different aspects of the proclamation of the gospel than the White man has been familiar with, something that is orthodox even if not a habitual part of (Eastern) Orthodoxy? And how is one to navigate these questions? Are we being called from the "institutional" ecumenism of the past century to an "ecumenism of the Spirit" as argued here, and might this indeed be a particularly Pentecostal gift? These are indeed difficult questions, yet also necessary ones. If Pentecostalism is indeed, as has been widely reported, the largest and fastest growing Christian body today, Pentecostal orthodoxy will surely be a major force within world Christianity, and so its evolution and future developments or pathways are ones to be noted. And as the first attempt to characterize and so shape an emerging Afro-Latino Pentecostal Orthodoxy, this is a welcome book.

ACKNOWLEDGMENTS

THIS WORK HAS BEEN MADE POSSIBLE first and foremost because of God's grace and mercy and afterwards because of men and women who have believed and invested in me. To Bishop Troy Anthony Bronner (Dad), thank you for challenging me to believe in my abilities and for forming me to be the minister I am today. To Dr. Eldin Villafane, thank you for teaching me that education is as much a part of my calling as preaching and teaching. Because of you I am convinced that I was called to be educated. To Archbishop Wayne Boosahda, thank you for classically training me in the recovery of the Great Tradition. This book is the fruit of the vision God gave you concerning me many years ago. To Bishop David Michael Copeland, thank you for causing my heart to burn with the phrase, "Many people know Jesus, but they don't know the church." The phrase changed my perspective and set me on my course of discovery. To Dr. Dale Irvin, thank you for taking a chance on me when no one else would. Time and time again you have sacrificed your name and reputation in order to ensure that my voice is heard among important theological and ecclesiological conversations that you are having. I will forever be grateful.

To Dr. Dara Delgado, thank you for all the hours of conversation regarding this work, and thank you for challenging me. I can't wait for your work to be published. To Dr. Claudette Copeland (Mother), thank you for loving me how only a mother can. I am uplifted by your prayers. To Fr. John Behr, thank you for fanning the flames of my passion for the patristics. I look forward to this next season of life under your tutelage.

A special thank you to the best church anyone could pastor, The Cathedral at the Gathering Place in Rochester, New York. Thank you all for your patience, devotion, and belief in the vision that God has given to us. As we like to remind each other, I've seen him do it and I know he's working it out for me!

To the clergy and people of the Union of Charismatic Orthodox Churches, thank you for supporting me as your leader. As we work together to recover the Great Tradition in order that we might help to renew the contemporary church, I look forward to your growth and vitality.

To bishops Johnny Ray Youngblood and Ronnie Eggleston along with Mount Pisgah Baptist Church and Ephraim Judah Cathedral, words cannot describe the immense love and respect I have for you all. Thank you for loving me unconditionally. I love you all.

Lastly, to my kids, Eli, Siomara, and Lucas, my babies. Thank you for being so patient with Daddy. After God, you guys are the sole purpose for my continuing existence. Daddy loves you!

INTRODUCTION

ONE EARLY SATURDAY MORNING in 2007, I was sitting in my prayer room, sobbing like a child. I had intended to pray the daily office, using my newly found appreciation for the Book of Common Prayer. But instead my mental fatigue had triggered my bipolarism, causing an avalanche of thoughts to come crashing down on my mind. The night before I had stayed up late reading Yves Congar's *The Meaning of Tradition*, along with Alexander Schmemann's *The Eucharist*, both a part of my formational training for the diaconate.[1] Just a year ago I had been a young, fiery Pentecostal minister who never expected to be thinking about matters of ecclesiology or tradition—or, for that matter, the Eucharist. The Eucharist? How and when did Communion become the Eucharist?

Those nostalgic thoughts of the distance between my younger years as a fiery, classical Pentecostal preacher on the traveling circuit and the man now sitting in a room with incense smoking, candles lit, prayer book in hand, and looked on with suspicion by some of the very people I had preached for caused me to begin to sob uncontrollably. I was not sad about the distance between my past and newly found way of liturgical prayer. In fact, after discovering so much historical, biblical, and ecclesiological truth,

---

[1]Yves Congar, O. P., *The Meaning of Tradition*, trans. A. N. Woodrow (San Francisco: Ignatius Press, 2004); Alexander Schmemann, *The Eucharist: Sacrament of the Kingdom*, trans. Paul Kachur (New York: St. Vladimir's Seminary Press, 2003).

how could I ever go back? However, my rediscovery of the truth of the early church's worship and theology came with a weighty price. Accusations stemming from a misplaced Catholo-phobia had distanced friends, colleagues, even family members, and on that particular morning, it had finally taken its toll on my mental and emotional health.

Back then, in 2007, I had already read Robert Webber's *Evangelicals on the Canterbury Trail*, in tandem with Thomas Howard's *Evangelical Is Not Enough*.[2] Those books were first recommended to me by the late Rick Hatfield, a priest in the Charismatic Episcopal Church who had taken the time to help me discern my new passion and interest for all things liturgical and sacramental. After months of conversation, it was Hatfield who was the first to tell me, "I think the Lord is calling you into convergence" (i.e., the convergence worship movement). A few months after making that statement, Hatfield suddenly became ill and passed on to be with the Lord.

Based on my reading of these books, I knew that if God was calling me to rediscover the historic Great Tradition (the worship, theology and mission of the church catholic found within scriptural exegesis, the church's creeds and councils and the writings of the Fathers within the first thousand years of Christainity), I would have to make the journey Webber describes from "Borrowed Faith, to Searching Faith, ultimately ending up at Owned Faith."[3] What I had not expected was the mental, emotional, and spiritual stress of it all. So there I sat, on the floor, mind racing, prayer book in hand, tears running down my cheeks as the realization of fleeting relationships and ministerial marginalization finally sunk in.

God has always had a peculiar way of revealing his love for me. As a child, I can remember vivid images of fiery plants and strange bright lights along with odd but divine encounters with beings, which I would later discern to be angelic. Rarely, however, did I have the experience of hearing a voice similar to how the book of Acts describes Paul's conversion encounter on

[2]Robert E. Webber, *Evangelicals on the Canterbury Trail: Why Evangelicals Are Attracted to the Liturgical Church* (New York: Morehouse, 2013); Thomas Howard, *Evangelical Is Not Enough: Worship of God in Liturgy and Sacrament* (Nashville: Thomas Nelson, 1984).
[3]Webber, *Evangelicals on the Canterbury Trail*, 3.

the Damascus road. So you can understand how the following came as a shock to me. The room had no windows, yet as I sat, struggling my way through prayer, I suddenly felt as if the sun's warmth had surrounded me. The light coming from the lit candles seemed to dim in the presence of a new and brighter light that had invaded the room, and the incense's smell increased dramatically. Then, without warning, I felt it: the strange sensation of a warmth covering my whole body, and in an instant I knew the manifested presence of the Holy Spirit was there. I later came to recognize that my experience that day was similar to Saint Symeon the New Theologian's ecstatic experience with the Holy Spirit as light in the tenth century.

I continued in prayer, still experiencing these sensations, until suddenly out of nowhere a picture of a friend popped up in my mind's eye, as if I were being shown a mug shot. I wondered for a moment whether God wanted for me to pray for that individual, and so, in spite of the emotional and ecstatic moment that I was having, I attempted to momentarily put aside my own awe and emotional malfunction. I began to prepare myself to pray for that friend. Suddenly, I heard a voice in my heart that asked, "Do you know him?"

Still with the picture in mind, I responded to the voice. "Yes, Lord, he's my friend. I know him."

There was silence for a minute or two, and then the voice spoke again. "What's his wife's name?"

I was stumped. I tried to recall the times and places where this individual and I had seen or spoken to each other, at conferences or other social or religious events, and after several minutes, having thought hard, I replied, "God, I don't think I know his wife."

Again, silence, until the voice asked, "How can you say you know him if you don't know the very thing he loves?" As I sat there puzzled, wondering what any of this had to do with my feelings of loss regarding my recovery of early Christian spirituality, I heard the voice once again asking, "Son, do you know me?"

By this time my suspicion has been elevated to code-red status. I figured that any answer to the question would probably be wrong, and yet I responded, "God, I try to know you every day as best as I can. I know that no one can completely know you, but I try."

Then the voice asked, "Do you know my bride, the church? How can you say you love me if you don't know what I love?"

□□□□□□

Thirteen years removed from that experience, I can truly say that I have learned how to love both the Groom and the bride. What's more, the re-telling of my story today does not seem as unique as it once did, amid the dozens of testimonials I've received from other Pentecostal clergy who have had similar experiences. As an Afro-Latino Pentecostal clergyman and religious educational scholar whose spirituality includes the recovery of the Great Tradition, it no longer shocks me to be seated on a plane or in a car next to a charismatic or Pentecostal person who expresses their desire for the recovery of some type of early Christian spirituality, inclusive of the Eucharist. These experiences seem to be the norm for Pentecostals who are transitioning from a pure fundamentalist evangelical Christianity into the recovery and practice of classical consensual Christianity. As I reflect back on that season of my life, I have come to believe that part of my difficulty at the time was that I knew no one else with my skin color who spoke my cultural language or worshiped charismatically, as I did, who was going through a similar transition. It was only years later that I met others who had similar stories.

Even more troubling was that while studying I began to notice that not only were the majority of my assigned readings written by older white men, but most of the personal stories concerning a dramatic conversion experience toward the recovery of the Great Tradition were being told from a primarily evangelical perspective. My remarks here concerning the overwhelming Anglo contribution toward the subject should in no way be taken as disparaging the incredible work done by my fellow Anglo brothers and sisters. In truth, this work itself is owed to individuals such as Webber and Thomas Oden, who set the pace for both the theological and pastoral recovery of classical consensual Christianity. Yet now more than ever I understand that the lack of cultural diversity pertaining to the subject continues to perpetuate a great social-religious chasm between Afro-Latino Pentecostals and historic Christianity.

Given the growing number of Pentecostals currently going through the process of recovering the faith and spiritual practice of the Great Tradition, a book addressing this topic is needed now more than ever before. The discussion itself, however, is complex and evolving. Therefore, prudence demands that, before I continue, I clarify what this book is and is not. It is not a catalog of global Pentecostalism and its various identities or denominations in relation to orthodoxy. It is also not my theological *summa*, although it is in some ways theological. Nor does the book focus on the sociopolitical or socioreligious distinctiveness of Blackness or brownness as identities or symbols, even though this topic will be discussed in chapter five.

This book is first of all an attempt to bring attention to a largely unknown and underconsidered but growing segment of North American Pentecostalism that is slowly moving away from a fundamentalist evangelical way of being in the world and shifting toward the faith and practice of a more liturgical, sacramental, and creedal Christianity. This shift is the sole work of the Holy Spirit, aided by a theological recovery of early Christian resources in tandem with an appreciation for liturgical experientialism as religiously educational.

Second, this work looks to problematize the sometimes-popular notion that orthodoxy and Pentecostalism are antithetical. In doing so, it will highlight both the various theological/academic resources within Pentecostalism that have been moving toward the recovery of the Great Tradition and the ecclesiological movements within the same that practically embody said recovery. It looks to join and colorfully contribute to the growing chorus of ancient-future literary voices that have both identified and mapped the growing number of nonliturgical Christian believers who are recovering the treasures found in the ancient wells of the Great Christian tradition.

Last, this work will consider the theological and historical qualifications for an orthodox Pentecostalism, situating it within the postmodern paleo-orthodox movement. It will consider how Afro-Latino Pentecostals are contributing to the social-religious chasm between Afro-Latino Pentecostals and historic Christian spirituality. The majority of these voices have, until now, been dominated solely by a white evangelical denominational presence. It will also consider the effects that such a movement within a broader global Pentecostalism could have on ecumenism. Further, one of the aims of this work is to introduce Pentecostals to the recovery of orthodoxy without displacing them from their Pentecostal tradition. In doing so, I hope it will become an encouraging and formational resource to both present and future generations of Pentecostal believers who sense a call to the belief and practice of the Christian faith believed "everywhere, always and by all."[4]

Whatever your own theological and ecclesiological perspective, my hope is that this book will be discussed, debated, and ultimately improved on.

TERMINOLOGY

This work uses the term *Pentecostal* to refer to the twentieth-century North American movement rooted not only in Wesleyan and Holiness spirituality but in African American spirituality as well. Following Douglas Jacobsen's research, what constitutes Pentecostalism is an experiential spirituality that is Spirit-filled and endows Pentecostal believers with the gifts of the Holy Spirit toward the miraculous. Pentecostal spirituality is deeply eschatologically minded and is heavily involved in the belief of spiritual warfare against the demonic in the world. In regard to gender and cultural equality, Pentecostal theology affirms that the Holy Spirit can empower women the same as men, and in practice has been open to peoples of all cultures. Concerning structure, Pentecostalism has no central governing body or authority; instead, it represents a grassroots entrepreneurial ecclesial movement of believers who share the Holy Spirit's work in the world.[5]

Jacobsen, as well as Allan Anderson, attests to the reality that ministry leadership within Pentecostalism is viewed more through the lens of a spiritual call and less through intellectual or academic preparation and

---

[4]Vincent of Lérins, "The Commonitory of Vincent of Lerins," trans. Charles A. Heurtley, in *A Select Library of the Nicene and Post-Nicene Fathers of the Christian Church*, 2nd ser., vol. 11, ed. Philip Schaff and Henry Wace (1885–1887; repr., Peabody, MA: Hendrickson, 1994) chap. 2.6.

[5]See Douglas Jacobsen, "The Pentecostal/Charismatic Tradition," in *The World's Christians: Who They Are, Where They Are, and How They Got There* (Malden, MA: Wiley-Blackwell, 2011), 50-61.

further that the doctrine of "the Priesthood of all believers constitutes a dynamic which serves as the missional impulse of the movement."[6] In this manner, the massive and diverse bodies of peoples within Pentecostalism are held in relation to one another, given mutual awareness, and cause for collaboration, and to the same extent they have begun participating in ecumenical dialogue with other traditions.

The classical, older Pentecostal doctrine holds that although every believer at conversion is baptized into Christ (justification), they are not necessarily baptized into the Spirit, that speaking in tongues is a sign of such baptism in the Spirit, and that eternal security or the assurance of salvation does not exist.

The term *Pentecostal* is also used, to quote Amos Yong, as a "catch-all, neo-charismatic" category within Pentecostalism that "comprises 18,810 independent, indigenous, post-denominational groups."[7] This neo-charismatic or neo-Pentecostal movement, as identified by *The New International Dictionary of Pentecostal and Charismatic Movements*, is distinct from the classical Pentecostal movement that was connected to the Azusa Street revival in the early 1900s.

Neo-Pentecostalism is also distinct from the charismatic renewal movement, which began within Protestantism but had a major effect among laypeople in several Christian traditions, including Roman Catholicism and Anglicanism, in the mid-1960s.[8] Charismatics not only believe it is possible to be baptized in the Spirit without speaking in tongues but usually espouse a broader ecumenical ecclesial pneumatology that shuns the need for separation among denominations. They do "share a common emphasis on the Holy Spirit, spiritual gifts, Pentecostal-like experiences along with signs and wonders and power encounters."[9]

---

[6]Allan Anderson, *An Introduction to Pentecostalism: Global Charismatic Christianity* (New York: Cambridge University Press, 2004), 243-60.

[7]Amos Yong, *The Spirit Poured Out on All Flesh: Pentecostalism and the Possibility of Global Theology* (Grand Rapids, MI: Baker, 2005), 18.

[8]"Introduction," in *The New International Dictionary of Pentecostal and Charismatic Movements*, ed. Stanley M. Burgess and Eduard M. Van Der Mass (Grand Rapids, MI: Zondervan, 2002), xix-xxi.

[9]"Introduction," *New International Dictionary of Pentecostal and Charismatic Movements*, xx.

Stanley Burgess argues that a distinction must be made between the terms *Pentecostal* and *Pentecostalism*. The term *Pentecostal* is limited primarily to classical Pentecostals, who emphasized the importance of the historical practice of speaking in tongues, while *Pentecostalism* describes a more general movement that recognizes the presence of spiritual gifts within a worship experience as described in the New Testament Scriptures.[10] Pentecostalism has always been a significant movement within the church. Moreover, a historical mapping of the movement reveals that, "For the first two centuries of the Christian era, there is abundant evidence of ongoing Pentecostalism."[11] Pentecostalism, then, according to Burgess, has "never lapsed, it has never ceased to be an ecclesial-pneumatological reality. It did not expire at the close of the first century until it was once again recovered in 1906 at the Asuza Street Revival as some Classical Pentecostals have suggested."[12]

Amos Yong offers a different perspective on Pentecostal terminology. Yong acknowledges that "Pentecostalism is, has been, and will be a contested idea," but unlike Burgess, he uses the terms *Pentecostal* and *Pentecostalism* (capitalized) when referring to the classical expression, which focused on speaking in tongues.[13] In contrast, he uses the terms *pentecostal* and *pentecostalism* (lowercase) to refer to the historic movement in general, inclusive of the three types of Pentecostalism described by the *New International Dictionary of Pentecostal and Charismatic Movements*.[14]

Similarly, Douglas Jacobsen and James Smith have, according to Smith, "adopted the nomenclature of 'small-p' pentecostalism as a way of honoring the diversity of pentecostal/charismatic theologies while at the same time recognizing important family resemblances and shared sensibilities."[15] Smith, however, contrary to Yong, identifies himself as a charismatic and not a Pentecostal, and thus utilizes *Pentecostal* (capitalized) to also refer to

---

[10]Stanley M. Burgess, *Christian Peoples of the Spirit: A Documentary History of Pentecostal Spirituality from the Early Church to the Present* (New York: New York University Press, 2011), 4.

[11]Burgess, *Christian Peoples*, 4.

[12]Burgess, *Christian Peoples*, 4.

[13]Yong, *Spirit Poured Out*, 18.

[14]Yong, *Spirit Poured Out*, 18

[15]James K. A Smith, *Thinking in Tongues: Pentecostal Contributions to Christian Philosophy* (Grand Rapids, MI: Eerdmans, 2010), xvii.

the charismatic traditions. He acknowledges that the term *pentecostal* or *pentecostalism* (uncapitalized) "is meant to be a gathering term, indicating a shared set of practices and theological intuitions that are shared by Pentecostals, charismatics, and 'third wavers.'"[16]

Thus far, the terms have been capitalized out of respect for the broader tradition. From here throughout however, this study will follow Yong's methodology, using the terms *pentecostal* or *pentecostalism* (lowercase) to refer specifically to a North American ecumenical pentecostalism in interconnection with orthodoxy. These terms are inclusive of the neo-charismatic groups as well as the classical and mid-nineteenth-century Pentecostals. The term *pentecostal* will be used in conjunction with the term *orthodoxy* as a qualifier for *orthodoxy* to argue that both a spirituality and a theology of signs and wonders have always existed as part of the historic apostolic tradition.

By the term *orthodoxy*, I do not mean the Eastern Orthodox Church (capital O), but what Thomas Oden identifies as the "integrated biblical teaching as interpreted in its most consensual classic period." For Oden, it refers to a classic textual tradition that

> encompasses both Eastern and Western Christianity. Lowercase *orthodoxy* is a term not limited to any particular history of Greek, Antiochene, Syriac, Armenian, Mar Thoma, or Coptic Orthodoxy, although it certainly includes all of these. I speak of lowercase orthodoxy as a sociological type, while greatly respecting the historical rootedness and durability of its capitalized form.[17]

This consensual classical period spans the first thousand years of the church, before the Great Schism. Here *orthodoxy* is not limited to right teaching and belief in the theological sense but is inclusive of a practical pastoral dynamic as well. From this perspective, orthodoxy is the recovery of ancient scriptural interpretation and teaching, the usage of tradition as a faithful recollection of Scripture, the recovery of both writings of the earliest Christian writers (fathers, doctors, and theologians of the church) and a creedal and consensual identity, and, last, a renewed liturgical/sacramental spirituality with a recovered devotion for the Eucharist taking center stage.

---

[16]Smith, *Thinking in Tongues*, xvii.
[17]Thomas C. Oden, *The Rebirth of Orthodoxy: Signs of New Life in Christianity* (New York: HarperCollins, 2003), 29, 15.

According to Leslie K. Best, the term *Afro-Latino* is used to identify "a person who is Latino and of African heritage."[18] Alejandro de la Fuente and George Reid Andrews define the field of Afro-Latin American studies "first as the study of people of African ancestry in Latin America, and second, as the study of the larger societies in which those people live."[19] This book uses the term *Afro-Latino* in the second sense, as a collective, sociologically referring to a group or community of both African Americans, Latino Americans, or Latinos with African descent in social motion.

This term stems from the reality of racial disparities for African Americans as well as Latinos in the United States, which are often interrelated. This has been particularly true in the southern states. Ramona Houston states, "Throughout its history, African Americans and Latinos have been subjected to similar forms of racialization, segregation and discrimination which in turn, have produced some of the same social, political and economic issues within each of these communities."[20] Houston's call is for an Afro-Latino coalition based on intergroup commonalities that supports collaboration between the two groups. Thus, given the similarities of racial and social designation, one can speak of an Afro-Latino community as a group of people who are either African American or Latino American with African heritage. I will provide a more concise definition of the term and how it is used in chapter five.

Finally, the term *Pentecostal orthodoxy* is used to refer to a segment of the broader pentecostal movement that is recovering classic consensual Christian teaching, along with elements of liturgical/sacramental worship, while retaining an affective spirituality and theology. My use of the term "affective spirituality and theology" means to suggest, straightforwardly, Theodore Runyon's understanding of John Wesley's Christian experience as *orthopathy*.[21] For Dale Coulter, orthopathy describes "how right

---

[18]Leslie K. Best, *The Afro-Latino: A Historical Journey* (Matteson, IL: Besslie Books, 2010), vii.

[19]Alejandro de La Fuente and George Reid Andrews, *The Making of a Field: Afro-Latin American Studies; An Introduction* (New York: Cambridge University Press, 2018), 1.

[20]Ramona Houston, "The Value of African American and Latino Coalitions to the America South," *The Journal of Global Initiatives: Policy, Pedagogy, Perspective* 2, no. 1 (June 2010): 65, https://digital commons.kennesaw.edu/cgi/viewcontent.cgi?article=1019&context=jgi.

[21]Theodore Runyon, "A New Look at Experience," *Drew Gateway* (Fall 1987): 44-55; Theodore Runyon, *The New Creation: John Wesley's Theology Today* (Nashville: Abingdon, 1998).

affections fuse right beliefs (orthodoxy) and right practices (orthopraxis) within Wesley's thought."[22] Importantly, members of this segment are usually more inclined to stay within their own Pentecostal tradition, incorporating and contextualizing the theology and spirituality learned, rather than joining a historic mainline liturgical tradition.

ORGANIZING THIS BOOK

This book makes the bold claim that, through an ecumenism of the Spirit, segments of Pentecostalism have been given the opportunity to recover the Great Tradition. I will argue that, unlike other Protestant movements before it, Pentecostalism as a multidiverse religious category can situate its spirituality, ministry, and theology within the broader mystical and monastic Christian traditions. Pentecostal orthodox ecclesiology, however, must be situated as an expression within the broader paleo-orthodox Christian movement, which includes other expressions, such as evangelical orthodoxy, the ancient-future movement, and the convergence worship movement.

In chapter one, "Reconstructing Foundations," I present a short developmental history of the paleo-orthodox movement along with its key expressions, characters, events, and literature. I reconsider the traditional historical outline compiled by other resources in regard to the amalgamation of the liturgical/sacramental, evangelical, and charismatic/Pentecostal streams of the church, aiming to present a broader narrative of the shift among Protestants that ultimately leads to a Pentecostal orthodoxy. The chapter concludes by analyzing why Pentecostalism has never been considered orthodox.

In chapter two, "Can Anything Orthodox Come from Pentecostalism?," I will look to answer the question posed in the preceding chapter: "Can Pentecostalism be orthodox?" The chapter's title, utilizing a play on words from the conversation between Nathanael and Philip in John 1:46, will present a scholastic and ethnographic research study of Pentecostal academic resources, churches, clerical organizations, and individual clergy

---

[22]Dale Coulter and Amos Yong, eds., *The Spirit, the Affections, and the Christian Tradition* (Notre Dame, IN: University of Notre Dame Press, 2016), 5.

drawn to the faith and practice of the Great Tradition. Inquiring who, what, where, why, and how, I first explore a Pentecostal orthodoxy by presenting a continuation of my own personal story as well as the stories of other Pentecostal clergy who have been drawn to the faith and practice of the Great Tradition. Second, the chapter explores the contrasts and comparisons between historical Pentecostalism and the Christian mystical tradition. Last, it reviews the history and ecclesiological developments of the clerical organizations that house Pentecostal clergy currently practicing forms of a Pentecostal orthodoxy. The overall aim of the chapter is to problematize the historical notion that Pentecostalism and orthodoxy are antithetical religious concepts.

Chapter three, "Pentecostals on a Pentecostal Trail," wrestles with the question of whether Pentecostals recovering the Great Tradition can or should remain within Pentecostalism instead of "coming home" to other canonical traditions upon such a recovery. After a brief consideration of the matter, I include a continuation of my own personal story and share the stories of three other pentecostals on a journey toward the recovery of the Great Tradition as well.

Chapter four, "Toward an Afro-Latino Pentecostal Orthodoxy," will explore an Afro-Latino Pentecostal perspective and the impact various forms of religious white normativity have had on the perception of Afro-Latino Pentecostal groups that are recovering a classical consensual Christian faith, believed to belong solely to "white" Christians. Guided by my understanding that my journey is no longer an isolated example of a broader phenomenon within Pentecostalism, one of the questions that must be asked is, Where are all the other Black and brown Pentecostal/charismatic people in this story? What is it about liturgy and sacramentality, in particular the Eucharist, in conjunction with early African Christianity, that has attracted Afro-Latino Pentecostals/charismatics to aspects of the Great Tradition? This chapter will argue that these Afro-Latino Pentecostal groups, aided by historical African Christian resources, are engaging in "colorful" or varied, fresh expressions of worship, situating an Afro-Latino Pentecostal orthodoxy within the broader Pentecostal orthodoxy movement.

Finally, chapter five, "An Ecumenism of the Spirit," presents readers with the ecumenical impacts that pentecostals recovering the Great Tradition can have on the "New Ecumenical Movement." This chapter contrasts the old ecumenism of the twentieth century as "a spiritual ecumenism" with the twenty-first-century, grassroots, Spirit-led ecumenical movement as "an ecumenism of the Spirit." It argues that a Pentecostal orthodoxy is part of the broader ecumenism of the Spirit and explores ways in which pentecostals recovering the Great Tradition can come to be seen as part of the one, holy, catholic, and apostolic church.

What a most wonderful time we live in as Pentecostal/charismatic believers. If you are a Pentecostal and you find yourself tired of solely identifying yourself with ripped-jeans, muscle-shirt preachers with $100 haircuts and heavily tinted beards; if you find yourself tired of moralistic therapy accompanied by emotional, performance-based worship devoid of godly and heavenly revelation; if you find yourself tired of the superficial and devotion to vestments, protocols, and ordinations with no connection to any historical or theological spiritual practice; if you yearn to discover the spiritual, contemplative, and theological writings of the Fathers and Mothers of the early church; if you find yourself frustrated with the lack of classical hermeneutical proximity as it relates to exegetical biblical preaching; if you find yourself desiring to renew your practice of a liturgical and sacramental spirituality inclusive of the Eucharist as the sacrament of the kingdom—then you are being drawn to the ancient wells of the Great Tradition. My hope is that as you read this book you will find the direction you need for your next season of ministry and personal spirituality.

1

RECONSTRUCTING FOUNDATIONS

OF THE MANY RESOURCES on the amalgamation of evangelical, charismatic/Pentecostal and liturgical/sacramental streams, few attempts have been made to offer a concise historical outline of the major expressions that encapsulate such spirituality.[1] Even fewer resources address how such expressions have contributed to segments of pentecostalism now looking toward the recovery of the Great Tradition.

This chapter looks to consider the history of the church expressions that combine the evangelical, liturgical, and charismatic streams of the church. These three streams, which to some extent can be seen being practiced in much of the early church, as illustrated in Lesslie Newbigin's book *The Household of God*, represent an outline that fits the practical and theological journey of pentecostals recovering the historic Great Tradition.[2] In truth, while other claims can be made in regard to other streams (e.g., the social justice stream), all Christian traditions will hold to, in one way or another, the existence of a charismatic, evangelical, or liturgical/sacramental element in their ecclesiology. I will examine three of these expressions in particular: evangelical orthodoxy, the convergence worship movement, and

---

[1]Gordon T. Smith, *Evangelical, Sacramental, and Pentecostal: Why the Church Should Be All Three* (Downers Grove, IL: IVP Academic, 2017); Winfield Bevins, *Ever Ancient, Ever New: The Allure of Liturgy for a New Generation* (Grand Rapids, MI: Zondervan, 2019).

[2]Lesslie Newbigin, *The Household of God: Lectures on the Nature of the Church* (Eugene, OR: Wipf & Stock, 2008).

ancient-future faith. These expressions will be situated within the broader paleo-orthodox movement and examined as antecedents to a Pentecostal orthodoxy. This work claims the paleo-orthodox movement as a valid, Protestant, theological, Spirit-led renewal movement dedicated to the recovery of the Great Tradition.

PALEO-ORTHODOXY

Since 1979, Thomas Oden has used the term *paleo-orthodoxy* to describe "an orthodoxy that holds steadfast to classic consensual teaching, in order to make it clear that the ancient consensus of faith is starkly distinguishable from neo-orthodoxy. The 'paleo' stratum of orthodoxy is its oldest layer. For Christians this means that which is apostolic and patristic."[3] Paleo-orthodoxy, or "ancient correct belief," refers to the late twentieth- and early twenty-first-century Protestant theological movement that sees the essentials of Christian theology in the consensual understanding of the faith as displayed within Christianity's first five centuries, the first seven ecumenical councils, and the writings of the church fathers before the Great Schism.[4] As a theological movement, it looks to critique the liberal rationalism and subjectivity of Christian modernity and to answer the questions of Christian postmodernity by recovering classical Christianity. John C. Peckham writes that paleo-orthodoxy looks to "encourage Protestantism (especially evangelicalism) to retrieve the orthodox consensus of Christianity, particularly that of the patristic tradition."[5]

The paleo-orthodox movement, along with its expressions (evangelical orthodoxy, convergence worship, ancient-future faith, Pentecostal orthodoxy), most commonly takes a communitarian approach to theology. Similar to the canonical approach, the communitarian approach sees the canon of Scripture as authoritative, yet emphasizes the authority of the Christian community in adopting what Peckham calls a

---

[3] Thomas C. Oden, *The Rebirth of Orthodoxy: Signs of New Life in Christianity* (New York: HarperCollins, 2003), 34.

[4] Kenneth Tanner and Christopher A. Hall, eds., *Ancient and Postmodern Christianity: Paleo-Orthodoxy in the Twenty-First Century* (Downers Grove, IL: InterVarsity Press, 2002).

[5] John C. Peckham, *Canonical Theology: The Biblical Canon, Sola Scriptura, and Theological Method* (Grand Rapids, MI: Eerdmans, 2016), 95.

"community-determined extracanonical rule of faith or other normative interpreter for theological doctrine."[6] An extracanonical normative interpretive arbiter is a way of interpreting Scripture and developing the authority of doctrine away from a solely scriptural (*sola Scriptura*) approach. It argues that community can also have a decisive say in the interpretation of Scripture and in developing authoritative doctrine.

This fact is significant for paleo-orthodox segments within Protestantism, since a community-determined extracanonical normative interpretive arbiter represents one way of thinking about a recovery of an ancient consensual method of interpreting Scripture. Roman Catholicism's communitarian approach to theological method, for example, involves its magisterium (teaching office) as its extracanonical normative interpretive arbiter, while Eastern Orthodoxy adheres to what it has come to know as "the rule of faith," which is a symbiotic relationship between the church, Scripture, and the apostolic tradition.[7]

In Protestant postliberal renewal movements such as paleo-orthodoxy, extracanonical normative interpretive arbiters also make meaning within the practices and faith of a believing community. Paleo-orthodoxy, in particular, adopts Vincent of Lérins's rule of faith—*ubique, semper, omnibus* (everywhere, always, and by all)—as its guide toward its consensual and Spirit-guided discernment of Scripture.[8] The Vincentian rule, according to Oden, is the "decisive text for orthodox ancient ecumenical method," because agreement at all three levels (that which has been believed everywhere, always, and by all) "assures reliable truth."[9] Oden's reliance on the Vincentian rule for the recovery of classical consensual Christianity is shared by many high-church Anglicans, and within Methodism (Pentecostalism's direct antecedent) John Wesley himself was influenced heavily by the Vincentian rule.[10]

---

[6]Peckham, *Canonical Theology*, 74.

[7]Peckham, *Canonical Theology*, 75-79.

[8]Peckham, *Canonical Theology*, 96.

[9]Oden, *Rebirth of Orthodoxy*, 157, 163.

[10]Albert C. Outler, in speaking of John Wesley's five principles of theological and biblical interpretation, states, "His last rule is actually a variation on the Anglican sense of the old Vincentian canon that the historical experience of the church, though fallible, is the better judge overall of Scripture's

While teaching at Drew University, Oden was challenged to study the classical writers of the Christian tradition by his Jewish mentor, Will Herberg. This led Oden to have what he describes as a radical "change of heart" regarding the importance of patristic intervention within modern and postmodern theology. Oden says, "Holding one finger up, looking straight at me with fury in his eyes, [Herberg] said, 'You will remain theologically uneducated until you study carefully Athanasius, Augustine and Aquinas.'"[11]

It was Oden who coined the term *paleo-orthodoxy*. For Oden orthodoxy is defined as "nothing more or less than the ancient consensual tradition of Spirit guided discernment of Scripture," which consists of the "integrated biblical teaching as interpreted in its most consensual classic period."[12]

Oden sees paleo-orthodoxy as a renewal movement emblematic of a new ecumenical reality that is a work of the Holy Spirit grounded in a personal faith in Jesus Christ. This movement can take a number of forms (Pentecostal, Catholic, Orthodox, or charismatic) and represents "a very deliberate, intentional ecumenizing of renewal movements."[13] In speaking of the terms "renewing church," "renewing Christians," and "renewing Christianity," Oden states that all "refer to a single movement that is full of vitality and touched with many features of spontaneity, charisma, and inspiration." Further, the term *movement* "does not yield easily to being described as a static object or an inert standing entity. . . . If it were not moving and changing it would not be a movement."[14] Oden's extensive theological body of work continues to inspire innovative and creative ways in which Protestants can think about the recovery of the Great Tradition.[15]

---

meanings than later interpreters are likely to be, especially on their own." See Outler, *John Wesley's Sermons: An Introduction* (Nashville: Abingdon, 1991), 67.

[11]Thomas C. Oden, *A Change of Heart: A Personal and Theological Memoir* (Downers Grove, IL: IVP Academic, 2014), 136.

[12]Oden, *Rebirth of Orthodoxy*, 24, 31, 129.

[13]Austin Welch, "Thomas Oden Interview on Church Renewal," *Juicy Ecumenism*, May 19, 2017, https://juicyecumenism.com/2017/05/19/thomas-oden-interview-church-renewal/.

[14]Thomas C. Oden, *Turning Around the Mainline: How Renewal Movements Are Changing the Church* (Grand Rapids, MI: Baker, 2006), 41.

[15]Oden's extensive work on the matter includes *After Modernity . . . What? Agenda for Theology* (Grand Rapids, MI: Zondervan, 1992); *Rebirth of Orthodoxy: Signs of New Life in Christianity* (New York:

Besides Oden, the most prominent contributor to the paleo-orthodox movement has been Robert Webber. In 1965 Webber, a Baptist fundamentalist, underwent a transformative shift in theological and ecclesiological thinking that ultimately led to his 1972 decision to enter the Episcopal Church. Fifteen years after Newbigin's *Household of God* and almost in parallel with Thomas Oden's work, Webber went on to chair the Chicago Call Conference, an appeal to evangelicals to recover an orthodox continuity with historic Christianity. As professor of theology at Wheaton College, Webber held a strong conviction that evangelicalism suffered from a reductionism in regard to historic faith and practice and thus had hoped that the Chicago Call would help "to restore a sense of historical awareness among evangelicals."[16]

As a distinguished evangelical scholar and former professor of theology at Wheaton College, Webber is credited with coining the phrase "ancient-future."[17] In calling for an evangelical appreciation of the historic Christian calendar, Webber remarks, "The road to the future runs through the past."[18] He valued a recovery of the Great Tradition among Protestantism, arguing that a return to classical consensual Christian truth possesses the power to speak to a postmodern world dissatisfied with the modern version of evangelical faith and with the current innovations that have no connection with the past.[19]

HarperCollins, 2003); *Classical Christianity: A Systematic Theology* (New York: HarperOne, 1992); *Change of Heart: A Personal and Theological Memoir* (Downers Grove, IL: IVP Academic, 2014); and last but certainly not least, his editing of the Ancient Christian Commentary on Scripture. Oden has also done extensive work in the rediscovering of early African Christian heritage, which has had a profound influence on current Afro-Latino ecclesial identity. Works written on the matter include *How Africa Shaped the Christian Mind: Rediscovering the African Seedbed of Western Christianity* (Downers Grove, IL: InterVarsity Press, 2007); *Early Libyan Christianity: Uncovering a North African Tradition* (Downers Grove, IL: IVP Academic, 2011); *The African Memory of Mark: Reassessing Early Church Tradition* (Downers Grove, IL: IVP Academic, 2011); and *The Rebirth of African Orthodoxy: Return to Foundations* (Nashville: Abingdon, 2016).

[16] Robert Webber and Donald Bloesch, eds., *The Orthodox Evangelicals: Who They Are and What They Are Saying* (Nashville: Thomas Nelson, 1978), 35.

[17] Webber was utilizing "convergence worship movement" until Leonard Sweet gave him the terminology "ancient-future."

[18] Robert E. Webber, *Ancient-Future Time: Forming Spirituality Through the Christian Year* (Grand Rapids, MI: Baker, 2004), 11.

[19] Robert E. Webber, *Ancient-Future Faith: Rethinking Evangelicalism for a Postmodern World* (Grand Rapids, MI: Baker, 1999), 29. His published works in ancient-future Christian spirituality have been acclaimed by Anglicans, evangelicals, and charismatics alike and include *Common Roots: The*

QUALIFYING CRITERIA FOR RENEWAL MOVEMENTS

Now that I have offered a brief introduction to the paleo-orthodox movement, it would behoove us to pause and reflect on whether the paleo-orthodox movement ought to be considered a valid Spirit-led renewal movement. If so, what definition exists for validating renewal movements? What are some of the qualifying criteria?

Donald A. Maxam defines church renewal in sociological terms as "individuals or groups who were implicitly or explicitly critical of the contemporary life, practice or thought of the Christian Church in the United States, and sought to work individually and corporately to change the church."[20] Similarly, Howard Snyder sees a sociological dynamic to renewal movements that operates as "God's work by his Spirit to create Christian community and to renew his people when they fall into unfaithfulness." These renewal movements, as opposed to church revivals, represent the inner dynamics of this work of the Spirit. As qualifying criteria, Snyder proposes that a renewal movement be a "theologically definable religious resurgence which arises and remains within, or in continuity with, historic Christianity, and which has a significant (potentially measurable) impact on the larger church in terms of number of adherents, intensity of belief and commitment, and/or the creation or revitalization of institutional expressions of the church."[21]

Snyder's definition and criteria for a renewal movement are significant when one considers that the historical analysis of his book covers Pentecostalism's ecclesial antecedents (pietism, Moravianism, and Methodism). For Snyder, these three religious groups, when examined under the lens

---

Original Call to an Ancient-Future Faith (Grand Rapids, MI: Zondervan, 2009); *Evangelicals on the Canterbury Trail: Why Evangelicals Are Attracted to the Liturgical Church* (New York: Morehouse, 2013); *Worship Old and New* (Grand Rapids, MI: Zondervan, 1994); *Ancient-Future Worship: Proclaiming and Enacting God's Narrative* (Grand Rapids, MI: Baker, 2008); *Ancient-Future Faith; Ancient-Future Time;* and *Ancient-Future Evangelism: Making Your Church a Faith-Forming Community* (Grand Rapids, MI: Baker Books, 2003). Webber also served as the main editor for *The Complete Library of Christian Worship*, 8 vols. (Peabody, MA: Hendrickson Publishers, 1995), a compendium for practical worship.

[20]Donald A. Maxam, "The Church Renewal Movement in Sociological Perspective," *Review of Religious Research* 23, no. 2 (December 1981): 195-204.

[21]Howard A. Snyder, *Signs of the Spirit: How God Reshapes the Church* (Eugene, OR: Wipf & Stock, 1997), 9, 34.

he provides, are renewal movements in the sociological and religious senses. A closer examination of Snyder's historical exploration in *Signs of the Spirit* reveals a deep appreciation for an ongoing pnuematological presence within the life of the church, which for Synder is inclusive of the charismatic renewal movement. One must wonder, however, why Snyder hardly makes mention of Pentecostalism, and whether he considers global Pentecostalism to be a renewal movement at all. These questions are probably best left for another work, more adept to covering such queries in full.

Snyder's definition serves this work as an effective blueprint for examining, identifying, and validating the paleo-orthodox movement as a genuine renewal movement within postmodernity. The first criteria given by Snyder is that of a resurgence of sorts that must take place within such a renewal movement. A renewal movement by nature is not something brand new but something that is being "re-newed," rising again into activity or prominence.[22] Therefore, for a renewal movement to be legitimate, there must be something that is resurging. So what is resurging or being renewed in the paleo-orthodox movement?

The first area of resurgence or renewal in the paleo-orthodox movement is the recovery of classical consensual teaching. Oden speaks of a "rebirth of orthodoxy," by which he means first and foremost the recovery of "integrated biblical teaching as interpreted in its most consensual classic period." This teaching can also be referred to as either ancient or classical consensual scriptural teaching and encompasses the first five centuries of the Common Era, inclusive of the translation and interpretation of Scripture by the earliest orthodox believers. For Oden, "No profound recovery of orthodoxy can occur apart from the recovery of its classic texts."[23] John Wesley, speaking of the same, states:

> The most authentic commentators on Scripture, as being both nearest to the fountain, and eminently endued with the Spirit by whom all Scripture was given... I speak chiefly of those who wrote before the Council of Nicea.

---

[22]*Merriam-Webster*, s.v. "resurgence (*n.*)," accessed March 31, 2022, www.merriam-webster.com /dictionary/resurgence.

[23]Oden, *Rebirth of Orthodoxy*, 29, 98.

But who would not likewise desire to have some acquaintance with those that followed them? With St. Chrysostom, Basil, Jerome, Augustine, and above all, the man of a broken heart, Ephraim Syrus?[24]

As opposed to the rebirth of orthodoxy occurring within other areas of people's lives, such as worship, the leading indicator of the rebirth of orthodoxy in the academy for Oden is the recovery of historical scriptural interpretation.[25]

The second area where there is a renewal or resurgence for paleo-orthodoxy is in the church's liturgy and sacramental spirituality (especially the Eucharist). If for Oden the rebirth of orthodoxy means the recovery of classical consensual teaching, then for Webber the rebirth of orthodoxy means the recovery of biblical and historical worship. Unlike Oden, Webber's focus within the Protestant recovery of the Great Tradition is mostly centered on worship, as displayed in his numerous writings, in particular *Worship Old and New* and *Ancient-Future Worship*. In *Worship Old and New*, Webber advocates for a blended (old and new) worship that "respects the tradition yet seeks to incorporate worship styles formed by the contemporary church." This type of worship is drawn from the historical worshiping community at large, looking sympathetically at liturgical worship as well as worship within the various reformational churches and beyond. As a practical matter, *Worship Old and New* focuses itself on the four acts of "entrance, service of the Word, service of the Eucharist and the acts of dismissal."[26] For Webber, these acts are performed in conjunction with the biblical narrative of the people of God's way of being and worshiping within both the Old and New Testaments. Furthermore, these four acts, according to Webber,

> draw the worshipper into the experience of symbolizing a relationship to God through a joyful entrance that brings the worshipping community into God's presence, the reading and preaching of Scripture that speak to felt needs, a Eucharistic response that celebrates Christ's healing presence at

---

[24]Thomas C. Oden, *John Wesley's Scriptural Christianity: A Plain Exposition of His Teaching on Christian Doctrine* (Grand Rapids, MI: Zondervan, 1994), 66.

[25]Oden, *Rebirth of Orthodoxy*, 97.

[26]Webber, *Worship Old and New*, 13-14.

the table, and a mission-oriented dismissal that sends the people forth into the world to love and serve the Lord.[27]

In both *Worship Old and New* and *Ancient-Future Worship*, worship—as a whole but in particular Protestant evangelical worship—must "do God's story." By this Webber means that worship must "connect creation with God's involvement in the history of Israel, with his incarnation, death, resurrection, ascension, eternal intercession, and coming again to establish his rule over all creation." In *Ancient-Future Worship* (written after *Worship Old and New*), this is done, first, by way of a worship that remembers its past through *historical recitation* of preaching, creeds, and songs, as well as through a *dramatic reenactment* of the Lord's Supper and other liturgical rites, which "draws the worshipper into the action, not as an observer but as a participant."[28] Second, a worship that does God's story *anticipates the future.* Webber calls for an appreciation of the divine design found in the creation liturgy as described in Genesis 1–3, arguing, "If the creation liturgy expresses a divine design to the whole created order, what does that say about worship? It says that worship is not thrown together, that it too, like the rest of creation, is ordered and reflects the divine design."[29] This divine design includes the keeping of a Sabbath as God's vision for the world and a recognition and appreciation of temple space along with holy living.

The second distinction made by Synder's definition of a genuine renewal movement is that whatever the resurgence is or whatever is being renewed must remain within and have continuity with historic Christianity. Here paleo-orthodoxy's adamant recovery of both classical theology and liturgical sacramental worship is made stronger by its use of the Vincentian rule ("everywhere, always, and by all") as its official extracanonical normative interpretive arbiter. The Vincentian method as a rule of faith aids adherents of paleo-orthodoxy in distinguishing, as Oden puts it, "fraudulent expressions of faith from true faith."[30] It does so by employing

---

[27]Webber, *Worship Old and New*, 14.
[28]Webber, *Ancient-Future Worship*, 71, 51.
[29]Webber, *Ancient-Future Worship*, 60.
[30]Oden, *Rebirth of Orthodoxy*, 161.

universality, apostolic antiquity, and conciliar consent within the historic community of believers (especially Christianity's first five centuries) as a criteria for discovering truth.

This new ecumenical methodology (universality, apostolic antiquity, and conciliar consent) provides paleo-orthodox Protestants with a guideline for dealing with theological and biblical disagreements. Per Oden, when disagreements arise, "the universal prevails over the particular, the older apostolic witness prevails over the newer alleged general consent, and conciliar actions and decisions prevail over faith-claims as yet untested by conciliar acts."[31] This methodology not only allows paleo-orthodoxy to meet Snyder's second criteria (historic Christian continuity), but, according to Oden, also makes room for "Orthodox, Catholics and Protestants . . . [who] despite diverse liturgical and cultural memories, find unexpected common ground ecumenically by returning to classic inter-preters of scripture texts that still stand as authoritative for teaching today."[32]

Third, Snyder says that a renewal movement must have a measurable impact on the broader church in regard to number of adherents and in-tensity of belief and commitment to the movement. Whether or not paleo-orthodoxy, along with a Pentecostal orthodoxy as one of its various expressions, will have such a such an impact long term must be mainly left up to future researchers to decide. But given both my experience and research on the future growth of Pentecostalism, I do anticipate that Pen-tecostal orthodoxy as an expression of paleo-orthodoxy can and will have a major impact on the broader Christian world, particularly by way of ecu-menism. Philip Jenkins, in speaking of Pentecostalism and its global growth and impact, suggests that, according to projections made by David Barrett and Teresa Watanabe, "Pentecostal believers should cross the one billion mark before 2050."[33] In contrast, the population of Eastern Or-thodox believers by 2050, according to Barrett in the *World Christian En-cyclopedia* (2001), will have "shrunk to less than 3 percent of the world's

---

[31] Oden, *Rebirth of Orthodoxy*, 171-72.

[32] Oden, *Rebirth of Orthodoxy*, 186.

[33] Philip Jenkins, *The Next Christendom: The Coming of Global Christianity* (New York: Oxford University Press, 2002), 9.

population. . . . In the worst-case scenario, the total number of Orthodox believers in the world by 2050 might actually be less than the Christian population of a single nation."[34]

This work will argue for an understanding of Pentecostalism as a biblical and historical spirituality (*charismata*) among "people of the Spirit."[35] It will also argue that this Pentecostalism can be best situated ecclesially within the mystical and monastic Christian traditions, especially Eastern Orthodoxy. If that is the case, there exists a strong correlation between Pentecostalism as a spirituality, Eastern Orthodoxy, and future demographic projections. If the Orthodox population is expected to shrink because of demographic changes and shifting cultural implications, then its mystical and monastic spirituality will shrink with it unless it is kept alive.[36] Here, a Pentecostal orthodoxy within a booming Pentecostal population has the potential to not only keep the Eastern mystical and monastic spirituality alive but to see it blossom.

Snyder's last criteria for a renewal movement is that it must create or revitalize institutional expressions of the church. Here one could point to both the various institutional organizations that embody elements of paleo-orthodoxy and to older and more established organizations that have been revitalized. Newer organizations such as the Charismatic Episcopal Church, the Communion of Evangelical Episcopal Churches, the Union of Charismatic Orthodox Churches, and to some degree the Joint College of African American Pentecostal Bishops have been created in order to practice the recovery, renewal, and rebirth of a particular theological or liturgical/sacramental stream in amalgamation with others.[37] As to revitalization occurring within older, already established organizations, the Anglican Church of North America is a good example. The Anglican Church of North America continues to be shaped by paleo-orthodox expressions that stem from Webber's work.

---

[34]Jenkins, *Next Christendom*, 111.

[35]A term utilized by Stanley M. Burgess.

[36]Jenkins, *Next Christendom*, 110.

[37]Most recently there has been another branch off the Communion of Evangelical Episcopal Churches called the Continuing Evangelical Episcopal Communion. See Continuing Evangelical Episcopal Communion, accessed November 13, 2021, https://ceec.church/.

Having situated paleo-orthodoxy as a valid renewal movement, before I turn to its various ecclesial expressions, I must offer a word concerning the tendency to become overreliant on or uncritical of the recovery of the Great Tradition as Oden and Webber present it. First, in analyzing their overall perspective on a return to patristic roots, many times there seems to be a resounding consensus for a Christian European universality devoid of ethnic or cultural presence. Admittedly, as alluded to earlier, Oden in his later years did develop incredible introductory works regarding the importance of Africa and African theology within ancient Christianity, but to some extent the European framework still exists. Vince Bantu, in making the case for a dominant Romanization of early Christianity, makes this clear when he states, "Despite the multiethnic and international presence of the universal church during the fourth century Eusebius presents the Christian faith as 'inextricably interwoven' with the Roman Empire as his construction of Christian identity became foundational for subsequent Western iterations of church history down to the present day."[38]

Adherents of paleo-orthodoxy, in particular Afro-Latino adherents of the pentecostal orthodox expression, should consider strongly Bantu's work and seek the benefits that come from examining a broader, more robust cultural study of the recovery of the Great Tradition inclusive of non-Eurocentric Christian identity, which stems from theological expressions developed in Africa, the Middle East, and Asia.[39]

Another criticism of the overreliance on how Webber and Oden present the recovery of the Great Tradition is that the paleo-orthodox framework can sometimes also seems to favor dialogue with Eastern sources over Western Roman Catholic or Protestant traditions. This type of thinking necessitates a corrective inclusive of both Roman Catholic and Protestant voices, as attested by Anglican-Orthodox, Lutheran-Orthodox, and Catholic-Orthodox ecumenical dialogues.[40] Further, in reading Oden and Webber's presentation

---

[38]Vince L. Bantu, *A Multitude of All Peoples: Engaging Ancient Christianity's Global Identity* (Downers Grove, IL: InterVarsity Press, 2020), 18.

[39]Bantu, *Multitude of All Peoples*, 72.

[40]Geoffrey Wainwright and Paul McPartlan, eds., *The Oxford Handbook of Ecumenical Studies* (New York: Oxford University Press, 2021), particularly chaps. 3 and 6, can serve as a great resource for those seeking more information on the various contributions made by various traditions to

of the recovery of the Great Tradition, it can come off as almost mythic, fantastic, or even bloodless due to its inattentiveness to the dynamics of power and oppression in its reconstruction of a consensual proto-orthodoxy. Missing are the accounts of the Donatist martyrs or the forceful and violent conversion of "pagans" in fourth-century Gaza. Both accounts have deep cultural, material, and political implications for how people of varying beliefs and cultures in the Christian tradition are viewed and treated, a subject that neither Oden's nor Webber's sanitized historical recovery acknowledges.

Here again, Bantu is correct when, in reflecting on how violence was perceived in a Constantinian Christian state, writes, "The sentiment that God uses Christian agents to carry out violent acts for divine purposes is one that is strongly rooted in the administration of Constantine and, more importantly, in the Christians who lauded his efforts."[41] The bloody history of the sometimes-brutal power and influence exercised by Roman emperors in attempting to settle theological disputes (e.g., the Nestorian and monophysite controversies), especially in Africa, has for many African Americans and Latinx Christians led to finding a better fit in the churches that came out of Chalcedon for the recovery of the Great Tradition, a topic which will be picked up in chapter four.

I begin by examining the seminal and foundational work of Lesslie Newbigin, from which most, if not all, of the paleo-orthodox movement's theological framework comes.

THE HOUSEHOLD OF GOD

Conceptual framework. Any conversation concerning three streams of renewal movements within the life of the church as an expression of the paleo-orthodox movement must include Lesslie Newbigin's *The Household of God: Lectures on the Nature of the Church.* Over sixty years ago, Newbigin (a bishop in the Church of South India) set out to answer the question, "By what is the Church constituted?"[42] He argues that the

---

matters of faith and doctrine and on the recovery of the Great Tradition via a "transconfessional" recovery of a "reconciled diversity."

[41]Bantu, *Multitude of All Peoples,* 17.

[42]Lesslie Newbigin, *The Household of God: Lectures on the Nature of the Church* (Eugene, OR: Wipf & Stock, 1953), 9.

church's nature is inherently *Protestant, Catholic,* and *Pentecostal.* For Newbigin, these three streams, fragmented by human sinfulness, will have to somehow be reconciled if the church is to succeed in its ecumenical and missional efforts in the world. His thinking is emblematic of the lived pastoral experience with the Church of South India, which was an amalgamation of Anglican, Congregationalist, Presbyterian, Methodist, and Reformed theology.[43]

Purpose. The purpose of Newbigin's work seems to be the continual development of a missional and ecumenical agenda connected to the question of ecclesial identity. To this end, Newbigin himself states that he will "refer to three such factors: the breakdown of Christendom, the missionary experience of the Churches in the lands outside of the old Christendom, and the rise of the modern ecumenical movement."[44]

Gifts. Although far more influenced by neo-orthodox thinking, Newbigin's work is an early developmental pattern for the three-stream expression found in paleo-orthodoxy. What is more, by placing Pentecostalism with the other designations, he provides one of the first instances where Pentecostalism is set side by side as an ecclesial designation with Catholicism and Protestantism in an effort to answer the question of the church's constitutional nature. In describing the three-streams formulation, Newbigin reveals the prevailing thought of the 1950s, when Pentecostalism was viewed as a "third force."[45] He calls for a clear distinction between Protestant and Pentecostal identities, a perspective that I will explore further in the proceeding chapters.

Limits. In describing the first two streams by which the church is constituted (Catholic and Protestant), Newbigin qualifies the usage of the terms by conjoining the word *orthodoxy* to them. In designating Protestantism as orthodox, for example, Newbigin closely ties the qualification to sixteenth-century Reformational demarcations: true preaching of the

---

[43]"History," Church of South India, accessed December 11, 2017, www.csisynod.com/aboutus
.php.

[44]Newbigin, *Household of God,* 11.

[45]The title "third force" is given to Pentecostalism in Henry P. Van Dusen, "The Third Force in Christendom," *Life,* June 9, 1958, 122.

word, along with the right administration of the sacraments.[46] In speaking of Catholicism as orthodox, Newbigin associates the term with the sacramental nature of incorporation into Christ's church and thus the participation in the very life of Christ. In Newbigin's examination of the third stream (Pentecostalism), which he sees as part of what constitutes the church, the orthodox qualification he ascribes to Catholicism and Protestantism is missing. Instead, Newbigin stresses Pentecostalism's reliance on the power and presence of the Holy Spirit, saying "that neither orthodoxy of doctrine nor impeccability of succession can take place of this." He also characterizes Pentecostalism as a stream running "outside" the broader ecumenical movement, where the church is present only through the recognizable power of the Holy Spirit. For Newbigin, this "Community of the Spirit," unlike Catholicism and Protestantism, is not concerned with what has been given and is now unalterable (sacraments and Scriptures). Instead, Pentecostals lay an independent stress "upon that which is to be known and recognized in the present experience—the power of the ever living Spirit of God."[47] Newbigin's reluctance to designate Pentecostalism as orthodox gives cause for further reflection and exploration of his claims concerning historical and theological Pentecostal suppositions in the face of postmodern neo-Pentecostal developments.

The classical Pentecostalism practiced and believed in the 1950s and '60s not only was considered an anomaly within the American social fabric but was a conservative and classical spirituality suspicious of anything outside its scope.[48] This type of Pentecostalism could in no way either be considered or even want to identify itself with "orthodoxy." This might explain why Newbigin's work seemingly makes no attempt to designate Pentecostalism as orthodox. Was Newbigin's intentional exclusion of the term *orthodox* emblematic of his assumption that

---

[46]John Calvin, *Institutes of Christian Religion* trans. Ford Lewis Battles (Philadelphia, PA: Westminster Press, 1997), 4.1.9. "Wherever we see the word of God sincerely preached and heard, wherever we see the sacraments administered according to the institution of Christ, there we cannot have any doubt that the Church of God has some existence, since his promise cannot fail."

[47]Newbigin, *Household of God*, 68, 87-88, 98.

[48]Vinson Synan, *The Holiness Pentecostal Tradition: Charismatic Movements in the Twentieth Century* (Grand Rapids, MI: Eerdmans, 1997), 205.

Pentecostalism lacks a concerted focus for either the sacramentalism or the message of the church? If so, could this assumption be reconsidered in light of recent developments in segments of neo-pentecostals recovering the Great Tradition? Furthermore, what historical developments can be traced from other, prior expressions that would indicate such a change within Pentecostalism?

Conclusion. Since its publication, *The Household of God* has been hailed by many within Protestantism as one of the pioneering works responsible for the various shifts within postmodern ecclesiological thinking, particularly among evangelicals and Pentecostals/charismatics. The book has sparked the further development of a number of efforts to develop an amalgamated ecclesiology. Due to these efforts, dozens of national and international ecclesial evangelical and charismatic bodies dedicated themselves to the practice of an amalgamated three-stream Christian identity. These organizations (some of which I will cover in the next chapter) have recovered historical, ecclesiological orthodoxy, which includes a sense of sacramentality, creedal identity, consensual authoritative teaching, and liturgical worship. They tend to follow the church's liturgical calendar (Western or Eastern), celebrate the Eucharist every Sunday, and use some type of historical prayer book as a guide toward the administration of the sacraments and the ceremonies of the church. As part of the various shifts in Protestant thinking, however, concerning ecclesiological identity, the original trifold terminology (Pentecostal, Catholic, Protestant) used by Newbigin and others to refer to the nature of the church has been reworked. Far removed from Newbigin's original denominational terminology, those within the paleo-orthodox movement most commonly utilize *evangelical* terminology when referring to Protestant, *charismatic* when referring to both charismatic and Pentecostal (a designation that needs to be further explored), and *liturgical/sacramental* when referring to Catholic aspects of the faith and practice.[49]

---

[49]Resources written under such new terminology include Richard Lovelace, "Three Streams, One River?," *Charisma Magazine*, September 1984, 8, and Gordon T. Smith, *Evangelical, Sacramental, and Pentecostal: Why the Church Should Be All Three* (Downers Grove, IL: IVP Academic, 2017).

Now that we have a framework for paleo-orthodoxy inclusive of Snyder's conceptual framework for a renewal movement, along with Lesslie Newbigin's ecumenical and ecclesial work in *The Household of God*, we can continue to explore and examine the three paleo-orthodox expressions that led up to a call toward a Pentecostal orthodoxy.

THE CHICAGO CALL AND EVANGELICAL ORTHODOXY

Conceptual framework. The *Chicago Call: An Appeal to Evangelicals* is a document that served as the outgrowth of the Chicago Call Conference, which was a gathering of evangelical leaders organized at an old Catholic retreat center outside Chicago in 1977. The conference's ecclesial outgrowth produced the evangelical orthodox expression. The conference, according to Webber, "urged evangelical churches to turn away from an ahistorical Christianity to recover new and enriching insights from the early church."[50] It was attended by forty to forty-five scholars, pastors, theologians, and students, mostly from various evangelical denominations. Only forty-two of the participants signed the Chicago Call statement, which was a compilation of eight calls preceded by phrases such as "we decry" and "we confess." These phrases were meant to set the tone of each appeal. The eight appeals that make up the Chicago Call are as follows:

- a call to historic roots and continuity
- a call to biblical fidelity
- a call to creedal identity
- a call to holistic salvation
- a call to sacramental integrity
- a call to spirituality
- a call to church authority
- a call to church unity

These eight sections, along with a personal account by Webber and two responses from two other participants, were later printed and published as *The Orthodox Evangelicals: Who They Are and What They Are Saying.* The

---

[50]Webber, *Ancient-Future Faith*, 26.

Orthodox Evangelicals later not only galvanized an official ecclesial body (the Evangelical Orthodox Church) but also became a theological blueprint for charismatics recovering the Great Tradition.

Purpose. The purpose of both the Chicago Call and the evangelical orthodox expression is to reengage and recover historic Christianity in order to regain and secure evangelicalism's spiritual health. David Neff (former editor in chief of *Christianity Today*) makes this point clear when, in speaking of the Chicago Call and its adherents, he argues, "The goal was not historical recovery but spiritual health, and that they believed the spiritual health of the evangelical movement would not be possible without a renewed understating of its place in the church catholic."[51] Webber himself, in calling evangelicals out of what he deems to be "popular evangelicalism," states:

> My conviction, and the subject of this writing, is that evangelicalism must mature into a truly biblical and historic faith, and that through this maturation, the replenishment of its tradition and the revitalization of its message will occur. This will not take place, however, without both a chastening and a renewing. The process necessitates a purging of our modernity and a return to Christianity in its historic form.[52]

Gifts. The Chicago Call and the evangelical orthodox expression are of vital importance for two reasons. First, they both share Newbigin's designation of an evangelicalism (Protestantism) as orthodox, which is representative of an evangelicalism in spiritual connection with, and in recovery of, the Great Tradition. Inadvertently, evangelical orthodoxy paves the way for a pentecostal orthodoxy in that if the designation *orthodox* can be given to evangelicals recovering elements of the Great Tradition, as Peter Gillquist suggests both with his involvement in the Chicago Call as well as in his book *Becoming Orthodox*[53], then the same designation can be utilized for pentecostals who are also recovering elements of the Great Tradition as well, since evangelicalism is diametrically distinct from pentecostalism.

[51]David Neff, "The Chicago Call: Catholicity Through History," in *Evangelicals and the Early Church: Recovery, Reform, Renewal*, ed. George Kalantzis and Andrew Tooley (Eugene, OR: Cascade Books, 2012), 126.
[52]Webber, *Common Roots*, 38.
[53]Peter E. Gillquist, *Becoming Orthodox: A Journey to the Ancient Christian Faith* (Chesterton, IN: Ancient Faith Publishing, 2009).

Second, the Chicago Call and the evangelical orthodox expression provide future expressions with an ecclesial blueprint (for better or worse) for how to mobilize themselves missionally and organizationally away from a solely academic identity. To this end, much is still to be examined and explored regarding the successes and failures of the Evangelical Orthodox Church.

Limits. The Chicago Call Conference did not live up to its originally intended end. Even to this present day there are those who continue to view it, as Michael Gallo once described it, as "a small puff of smoke on the theological horizon."[54] What was slated to be a call toward fundamental reforms, recovery, and redirection within contemporary Protestant evangelicalism seemingly turned out to be an exercise in futility. This common sentiment is shared by observers such as Donald Tinder, who in an article in *Christianity Today* called the conference "an ad hoc group of 46 comparatively unknown Christians."[55] Even Thomas Howard, one of the originators of the conference, admits that the call ultimately "came to virtually nothing."[56] That the Chicago Call itself did little if anything during its time to convince its constituency or, for that matter, the broader evangelical world of the need to rediscover orthodoxy is also a sentiment shared by Randy Sly. Sly, a former archbishop in the Charismatic Episcopal Church, describes the evangelical reception to the Chicago Call as "less than half-hearted."[57] Forty-two of the forty-five invitees signed on to the Chicago Call, and sadly only one representative was Roman Catholic, and there was no representation from the Orthodox Church, even though they had been invited.

The uneasiness within the conference itself became evident after the fact, when statements on the part of participants concerning unauthentic evangelical voices ran in parallel with terms such as "Anglo-Catholics" and

---

[54]Michael F. Gallo, "*The Chicago Call* Ten Years Later," *Touchstone Magazine*, Winter 1988, www.touchstonemag.com/archives/article.php?id=02-02-007-f.

[55]David Neff, "Together in the Jesus Story," *Christianity Today*, September 1, 2006, www.christianitytoday.com/ct/2006/september/10.54.html.

[56]Gallo, "*Chicago Call* Ten Years Later."

[57]Randy Sly, "Special Report," Catholic Online, 2008, www.catholic.org/national/national_story.php?id=27157.

"crypto-Greek Orthodox," directed primarily at conference organizers Webber, Howard, and Gillquist, who were considered to have "high church tendencies."[58]

The concern of a good majority of conference participants about an unadulterated evangelicalism is possibly best articulated by David Wells, professor of history and history of Christian thought at Trinity Evangelical Divinity School. Wells, one of the Chicago Call's most verbal critics, in responding to what he sensed was the display of evangelicalism co-opted by Anglo-Catholicism, stated that he

> cannot be persuaded that we would be substantially better off venerating Catholic saints than pretty starlets, or that sober-faced genuflectors and swingers of incense are much to be preferred to the vacant worshippers some of our churches are creating. This may be a time of small happenings, of pygmy spirituality, but a mass pilgrimage into the world of Anglo-Catholicism is not, with all due respect, what we need right now. Indeed, it is not what we need at any time.[59]

Aside from the charge of having high-church tendencies, there also existed cultural and gender diversity issues, which became immediate stumbling blocks for many. Out of the forty-five scholars involved in the conference, there were only four women. While all of the women ended up signing the Chicago Call's document, none of them were mentioned in the drafting of the calls themselves, nor were any of them included in the compilation of essays printed later.

Even more disappointing is that African American and Latino American evangelical groups had little or no representation. To this point, Elesha Coffman, assistant professor of history at Waynesburg University, states, "When examining the signatories of the Chicago Call, there is not a lot to report on the diversity front. Those who gathered at Cenacle Retreat Center in Warrenville in 1977 were practically all white men."[60] Similarly,

---

[58]Gallo, "*Chicago Call* Ten Years Later."

[59]David F. Wells, "Reservations About Catholic Renewal in Evangelicalism," in Webber and Bloesch, *Orthodox Evangelicals*, 214.

[60]Elesha Coffman, "The Chicago Call and Responses," in Kalantzis and Tooley, *Evangelicals and the Early Church*, 109.

Benedict Viviano, the only Roman Catholic participant, remembers the conference as "an elite appeal to an elite."[61] Sharon Gallagher, at the time editor of the *Christian World Liberation Magazine*, responded to Webber's press release in a note that was later discovered at the Billy Graham Center archives. She expressed concern over the Chicago Call, objecting to the lack of women on the planning board and going as far as to call it "gross."[62]

Conclusion. Amazingly, forty years removed from the gathering at an old Catholic retreat center outside Chicago, diverse forms of paleo-orthodoxy within Protestantism increasingly find guidance from the pages of *The Orthodox Evangelicals*. The racial, gender, and social insularity that characterized much of the Chicago Call, which had reverberating effects for decades, has not deterred postmodern evangelicals or charismatics from turning to *The Orthodox Evangelicals* in striving to recover elements of Christian orthodoxy considered to constitute the fullness of the church (*plene-esse*).[63]

Effects such as continuing racial insensitivity and the social exclusion of women were factors that for some time seemed to place the recovery of orthodoxy outside the grasp of minorities. These factors, however, have been somewhat overcome recently, by both women and racial minorities, within the charismatic and neo-Pentecostal orthodox movements. There significant consideration has been given not only to components of ecclesial orthodoxy whose roots are in Africa but also to the historical role of women in ministry, a factor that I will consider in chapter five.

Interestingly, Coffman makes the following mind-blowing statement: "It is possible to view this document as a call without response."[64] Her comment, which encapsulates the sentiment of some at the time, is worth

---

[61] Gallo, "*Chicago Call* Ten Years Later."

[62] Chicago Call, Collection 33, Billy Graham Center, December 2, 2009, www2.wheaton.edu/bgc/archives/GUIDES/033.htm. Also taken from Coffman, "Chicago Call and Responses," 110.

[63] *Plene-esse* is a term most commonly used for elements of the historic Christian Tradition such as the episcopate, which are thought of as making up its full being. Erwin Fahlbusch, "Episcopacy," in *Encyclopedia of Christianity Vol 2.*, ed. Geoffrey W. Bromiley, David P. Barret, and Jaroslav J. Pelikan (Grand Rapids, MI: Eerdmans, 2000), 108.

[64] Coffman, "Chicago Call and Responses," 108.

examination now, especially given the various ecumenical developments that have taken place within the last forty-plus years.[65] In assessing the future impact of the Chicago Call from another perspective, Gillquist contends that it "put Evangelical Christians on notice that it is indeed possible to be both Evangelical and historically orthodox."[66]

THE CONVERGENCE WORSHIP MOVEMENT

Conceptual framework. In 1984, *Charisma Magazine* published an article describing a movement among evangelicals that highlighted the recovery of liturgical/sacramental aspects within evangelical and charismatic services.[67] The article, somewhat reminiscent of Newbigin's *Household of God*, was written by Richard Lovelace and titled "The Three Streams, One River?" Lovelace, an original contributor to the Chicago Call, argued (as Newbigin had before him) for a united Catholic, evangelical, and Pentecostal/charismatic church. The language used by Lovelace (now far removed from the language of evangelical orthodoxy) was overwhelmingly well received, especially among evangelicals and charismatics who were themselves yearning to recover the orthodox faith of the early church. Many of these Christians had been exposed to either the charismatic movement, through the Vineyard movement with John Wimber in the late 1970s, or the liturgical renewal movement of the 1960s.

Ten years after Lovelace's article, in an article in Robert Webber's *Complete Library of Christian Worship*, Wayne Boosahda and Randy Sly developed one of the first historical and theological descriptions of the historical trajectory and beliefs of what has since come to be known as the convergence worship movement. Sly and Boosahda, the latter of whom is believed to have been the first to use the term *convergence* to describe the movement, used Psalm 46, the same text used by Lovelace. Key common elements of the convergence worship movement are:

---

[65]Robert Webber and Donald Bloesch, eds., *The Orthodox Evangelicals: Who they are and what they are saying* (Nashville: Thomas Nelson, 1978), 212-33.
[66]Gallo, "*Chicago Call* Ten Years Later."
[67]Lovelace, "Three Streams, One River?," 8.

- a restored commitment to the sacraments, especially the Lord's Table
- an increased motivation to know more about the early church
- a love for the whole church and a desire to see the church as one
- the blending in the practice of all three streams is evident, yet each church approaches convergence from a unique point of view
- an interest in integrating structure with spontaneity in worship
- a greater involvement of sign and symbol in worship
- a continuing commitment to personal salvation, biblical teaching, and the work and ministry of the Holy Spirit

Purpose. Heavily influenced by both the charismatic and the liturgical renewal movements, the convergence movement sought to "experience the fullness of Christian worship and spirituality" through the blending of the "essential elements in the Christian faith, represented by the three majors streams of thought and practice."[68] Although not openly recognized until about 1985, it continues to argue for an experiential Christian spirituality that is wholly evangelical, charismatic, and liturgical/sacramental. Its ecclesial impetus is derived from an interpretation of Psalm 46:4: "There is a river whose streams make glad the city of God, the holy place where the Most High dwells" (NIV). According to this interpretation, the city of God is the church, the rivers are the action and flow of God's presence through the church, and the streams are the varied expressions within Christendom that have splintered off throughout its historical development, enriching the church in their respective times but now returning to each other, or converging, into one experience. This converging or blending of these three streams is considered by those who practice the convergence movement as "the work of God the Holy Spirit imparting a spiritual operation of grace best captured in the vision of Psalm 46:4."[69]

In the early stages of the movement, Webber himself had begun to utilize the language of convergence in his writings, acknowledging, "The convergence worship movement has intentionally brought about a

---

[68]Randy Sly and Wayne Boosahda, "The Convergence Worship Movement," in *The Complete Library of Christian Worship*, vol. 2, *Twenty Centuries of Christian Worship* (Nashville: Star Song, 1994), 134.

[69]Sly and Boosahda, "Convergence Worship Movement," 134.

synthesis between the liturgical and contemporary worship renewal movements."[70] Eventually, however, Webber stopped using the term *convergence* for fear that the terminology was being co-opted by New Ageism and began to use the term "ancient-future" instead. Since then, the convergence worship movement, as part of the broader paleo-orthodox movement, has been hailed as an alternative to the divisive, stagnant, and monolithic ecclesial spirituality that has contributed to the current mistrust of Christian mainline institutions.

Gifts. In their assessment of the future of the convergence movement, Boosahda and Sly use Malachi 4:5-6, which has the spirit of Elijah returning the hearts of the fathers to the children and the hearts of the children back to the fathers, as an "expression of hope." Their interpretation of the text sees a "new spirit in the church which will turn the hearts of this generation of believers back toward the apostolic fathers and other who formed and fashioned vital faith in the centuries following the ascension of Christ."[71] Missing in Boosahda and Sly's interpretation of the text, and an even more crucial point, is that the hearts of the fathers will turn back to the children. The application here speaks of a contextual relevance that situates the fathers and mothers of the church comfortably within Christian postmodernity and demonstrates a dynamic tension. If the children represent a generation of believers who are turning their hearts back to the apostolic fathers, then the presence of apostolic fathers within the hearts of the postmodern children represents an ancient spirituality and theology that is increasingly becoming relevant.

Limits. One of the most significant challenges facing the convergence movement today is for its adherents to explain its distinctive historical development and amalgamated religious spirituality in a way that can be understood within mainline Christian churches as well as society as a whole. While the movement itself has gained thousands of followers, it is often grossly misunderstood, and convergence spirituality remains an

---

[70]Robert Webber, "What We've Learned Along the Way: Reformed Worship Through Twenty Years of Liturgical Change," *Reformed Worship* 77, September 2005, www.reformedworship.org/article/september-2005/what-weve-learned-along-way-reformed-worship-through-twenty-years-liturgical.
[71]Sly and Boosahda, "Convergence Worship Movement," 139.

enigma to most Christians from mainline traditions, whose spirituality is usually informed by one or two traditions at best but never three. This is due in part to the increasing need for solid scholarly contributions on the part of convergence practitioners. Those from within the movement have yet to contribute any major bodies of work that seek to define, develop, or qualify the movement in light of social, political, and theological shifts occurring within postmodernity. Second, to my knowledge there has never been a real attempt by any of the convergence movement's adherents to qualify or identify the term *charismatic* versus *Pentecostal*, a reality that has allowed for an undescribed amalgamation along with a need for a clear distinction of how the recovery of the Great Tradition affects both.

Conclusion. Most recently, it seems as though the actual convergence movement has lost much of the vigor it exhibited in the '80s and '90s. Today, few prominent national or international ecclesial bodies exist that actually use the term *convergence* to describe their identity, even though they might use the term to describe their spirituality. Even more telling is that, as scholarship and amalgamated spiritual practices arise from mainline Christian traditions, specifically Anglicanism and Methodism, the terminology used mostly by white evangelical charismatics (convergence) is being replaced by less polarizing terminology.

ANCIENT-FUTURE MOVEMENT

In welcoming the death of modernity's "triumvirate of individualism, rationalism and factualism,"[72] Webber produced several ancient-future faith works, published with Baker Books. For Webber, ancient-future faith was also a response to postmodernity that brought with it the burden of saying that "the road to the future runs through the past."[73] However, for classical Christianity to be effective in postmodernity, a shift in how evangelicals perceived historic Christian paradigms would be necessary. In his foreword to Webber's *Common Roots: The Original Call to an Ancient-Future Faith*, David Neff writes that in *Ancient-Future Faith* "Webber stressed paradigm

---

[72]David Neff, "Foreword," in Webber, *Common Roots*, 20.
[73]Webber, *Ancient-Future Faith*, 7.

thinking and showed how classical Christian theology, worship, spirituality, and mission were well suited to postmodern ministry."[74]

Conceptual framework. Just as Oden dealt with many of the theological woes within modernity, Webber, in structuring *Ancient-Future Faith* as a call to evangelicals toward the recovery of the Great Tradition, tackled many of the same biblical, theological, and pastoral challenges existing within postmodernity. *Ancient-Future Faith* acts as a correction to Christian rationalism and subjectivity and is structured "around the phenomenon of the origin of the Christian faith first," instead of the Scriptures, where evangelicals usually start.[75]

Purpose. The purpose of *Ancient-Future Faith* is not only to problematize the sometimes ahistorical evangelical concept of paradigmatic historical thinking but also to develop a grounded subjectivity "anchored in the revelatory experience of the early Christians."[76] Pragmatically, it can be described as a call to the recovery of historic Christian theology along with the blending of historic Christian worship, which causes one to taste the "communion of the fullness of the body of Christ."[77]

"Ancient-future" primarily speaks to the varied evangelical groups represented by their cultural and subcultural groups and divisions. Webber counts as many as fourteen evangelical denominational groups. The issue, according to Webber, is that evangelical Christianity demonstrates a kind of amnesia that has caused it to be sadly deficient of historical knowledge.[78] While attempts to trace evangelicalism back to the Protestant Reformation have been and will continue to be commendable, they are nonetheless ahistorical and often limited in their thinking of what it means to be evangelical within the church universal. Therefore, evangelicalism, in order to become historically sufficient, must respond to the call to a historic Christianity. This begins with the life and work of Jesus Christ; develops the

---

[74]Neff, "Foreword," 20.

[75]Webber, *Ancient-Future Faith*, 30.

[76]Neff, "Foreword," 7.

[77]Joan Huyser-Honig and Darrell Harris, "Robert E. Webber's Legacy: Ancient Future Faith and Worship," Calvin Institute of Christian Worship, May 18, 2007, https://worship.calvin.edu/resources/resource-library/robert-e-webber-s-legacy-ancient-future-faith-and-worship/.

[78]Webber references Bernard Ramm in Robert E. Webber, *Common Roots: The Original Call to an Ancient Future Faith* (Grand Rapids, MI: Zondervan, 2009), 39.

image, worship, spirituality, and mission of the church; and deals with the question of authority for proclamation and presence in the world.[79] This methodology of biblical interpretation situates the evangelical notion of Scripture within a historical framework that is connected to the historical hermeneutical proximity of the first six centuries of the church.

An ancient-future call to the recovery of historic Christianity is inclusive of the theology and order of worship as well. For Webber, to recover the theology of worship is to recover a classical worship that places the Old and New Testament in a dynamic tension that resembles the held tension between word and sacrament—the Old being preserved by the early church in the liturgy of the word, while the New is preserved in the liturgy of the sacrament.[80] Along with the recovery of the order of worship within the Christian calendar and the arts (which Webber describes mostly as symbolic communication), this type of recovery sees Christian worship as doing God's story.[81]

Gifts. The ancient-future movement is the arm of paleo-orthodoxy that seems most interested in the recovery, blending, and proper situating of classical Christian worship within postmodern evangelicalism. As such, Webber's theological body of work on worship, which includes his Twenty Centuries of Christian Worship series along with *Worship Old and New* and *Ancient-Future Worship*, presents evangelicalism with a stark reminder of the church's maxim *lex orandi, lex credendi, lex vivendi* (the law of prayer/ worship leads to law of belief, which leads to the law of living). Webber's examination and exploration of the recovery and blending of historic Christian worship has been institutionally and academically embodied in the Robert Webber Institute for Worship Studies, located in Jacksonville, Florida. The institute offers both a master's and doctorate in worship studies and targets students from all Christian backgrounds, with online and residency approaches to learning available.

In contrast to the convergence movement, which has a limited body of official theological work and has been relegated to a more pastoral

---

[79]Webber, *Ancient-Future Faith*, 59, 39, 31.

[80]Webber, *Ancient-Future Faith*, 103.

[81]Webber, *Ancient-Future Worship*, 29. Webber answers the question "What is worship?" by stating, "Worship Does God's Story."

movement of amalgamation of Christian streams, the ancient-future movement has produced a large body of theological work accessible to both movements. Today it is no strange thing to find books being written with the "ancient-future" demarcation. Books such as Kenneth Stewart's *In Search of Ancient Roots: The Christian Past and the Evangelical Identity Crisis* and Winfield Bevins's *Ever Ancient, Ever New: The Allure of Liturgy for a New Generation* have been instrumental in continuing the legacy of Webber's *Ancient-Future Faith.*[82]

Limits. Ancient-future faith seems to be a continuation of evangelical orthodoxy wrapped in different packaging. One must wonder whether the multicultural, ecumenical, and gender lessons of the Chicago Call Conference have been learned and rectified within the ancient-future faith movement, particularly for North American Anglicanism. Presently, the ancient-future faith movement has continued mostly among evangelical Anglicans.

Conclusion. Since the ancient-future movement primarily looks to call evangelicals to the recovery of historic Christianity, one must wonder what evangelicals today can learn from historic Christianity's theology or spirituality in regard to their present political and social plight. How can the recovery of historic Christian theology influence their perception on issues such as immigration reform, gender and racial equality, and nationalism?

PENTECOSTAL ORTHODOXY

Conceptual framework. History is replete with movements or expressions (social, economic, or religious) that have either inspired successive generations toward change or have themselves become distant memories of what used to be. The church's history is no different. Whether the future of a Pentecostal orthodoxy will be one of impact or one of social-religious implosion, I will leave for our future historians to debate. I remain convinced that what is presently at work within segments of pentecostalism recovering the Great Tradition is the work of the Spirit

---

[82]Kenneth Stewart, *In Search of Ancient Roots: The Christian Past and the Evangelical Identity Crisis* (Downers Grove, IL: IVP Academic, 2017); Bevins, *Ever Ancient, Ever New.*

and that it constitutes a real phenomenon that deserves attention and identification. The expression itself, although I've coined the term *Pentecostal orthodoxy* to describe it, originates with no one person, group, or system. Pentecostal orthodoxy to date has no centralized church hierarchy, has no major institutional authority aside from each organization's hierarchical structure, and has not adopted or developed for itself any historical confession. In fact, a Pentecostal orthodoxy differs from much of Pentecostalism in that while Pentecostalism historically is suspicious of creeds and confessions, a Pentecostal orthodoxy embraces a creedal identity.

After all is said and done, Pentecostal orthodoxy represents a broad phenomenon within what can be described as autocephalous segments of pentecostalism that have been recovering what I call elements of the Great Tradition (vestments, sacramental terminology, and so on) over the span of decades. Yet, no real attempt has been made to identify, bring correctives to, or develop the expression further using a pentecostal theological or ecclesial framework. To this work have I given my energy. My hope is that better minds will engage, critique, build on, and develop the work presented here and that the expression will not only outlive me but aid various Christian traditions (pentecostalism in particular) in the work of rediscovering treasures old and new.

A year or so after having completed my doctoral program, I found that the research for my dissertation on paleo-orthodoxy and religious education had left me uneasy about using certain terminology in order to describe my spirituality and ecclesial or denominational identity. In particular, I wondered whether the term *convergence* (which I had adopted) adequately captured the subtle but important theological, historical, and even racial nuances between the charismatic and Pentecostal movements and their recovery of the Great Tradition. While wrestling with this idea, a defining or clarifying moment came to me through a conversation with my father, who has been for many years a minister in one of the larger Pentecostal denominations. One morning, while having breakfast at his favorite restaurant, we began to reflect on Brant Pitre's book *Jesus and the Jewish Roots of the Eucharist* and its implications for pentecostals (particularly the belief in "real presence").[83] I shared with him my own work on orthodoxy in relation to pentecostalism and the Eucharist, and by the end of the breakfast, my father stared at me and asked, "Would you consider me to be orthodox?"

My father's question stirred in me a desire to explore and examine the implications of designating the phenomenon of pentecostals recovering the Great Tradition, a Pentecostal orthodoxy distinct from the various antecedent expressions within paleo-orthodoxy. My foundational framework for the expression, as limited as it may be, yields interesting facets of the expression's spirituality and theology, most of which stem from my own experience with the congregations I led, my research of other pentecostal organizations/churches coming into the recovery of the Great Tradition, and scattered research on topics that deal with said recovery within pentecostalism. This research has never been placed together in order to develop a better understanding or identification of the phenomenon—a challenge I now undertake.

Pentecostal orthodoxy is an emerging expression within the broader paleo-orthodox movement of pentecostal believers recovering the theological and spiritual riches of the great tradition. In particular, there is a renewal of the liturgical celebration of the sacraments, especially the weekly celebration of the Eucharist, along with the recovery of a more ancient way of interpreting Scripture. This recovery is also inclusive of the church's liturgical calendar, creedal identity, councils, and writings of the Fathers within the first five centuries. These segments of pentecostalism are being drawn and empowered by an ecumenism of the Spirit, which differs from the old spiritual ecumenism in that, while the latter was mainly exercised by the heads of Christian communions, the former is laity driven.

Pentecostal orthodoxy is committed to the development of a historic, educational, sacramental, and liturgical affective pentecostal spirituality (orthopathy) ahead of the development of a dogmatic, propositional pentecostal theology. Two major points must be made concerning this type of pentecostal orthodox spirituality. First, as already alluded to above, this

---

[83]Brant Pitre, *Jesus and the Jewish Roots of the Eucharist: Unlocking the Secrets of the Last Supper* (New York: Doubleday, 2011).

spirituality and its continued development occur within a pentecostal framework. A Pentecostal orthodoxy is not evangelical orthodoxy, the convergence worship movement, or ancient-future faith. Rather, this framework calls for a way thinking from within pentecostalism about the work of the Holy Spirit in interplay with sacramental imagination, producing a new way of being pentecostal in the world. Furthermore, in comparing and contrasting its antecedent expressions, a Pentecostal orthodoxy's social-religious history is distinct from the rest in that its spirituality and ministerial presence is inclusive of minorities, people of color, and women. As a result, most adherents of the expression resist all calls to join the canonical churches. Instead the argument that I myself hold to and most commonly hear from adherents of a Pentecostal orthodoxy is that, just as those within the sacramental traditions (Anglicans, Roman Catholics, Lutherans and Eastern Orthodox) retained their identities after having recovered the baptism of the Holy Spirit during the charismatic renewal movement, pentecostals recovering the liturgical and sacramental elements of the Great Tradition should be allowed to retain their identity as pentecostals as well.

Second, a pentecostal orthodox spirituality looks to specifically and intentionally situate itself within the broader Christian monastic and mystical traditions. In regard to the former, the expression itself has more in common with the ascetic monastic spirituality of the fourth and fifth centuries, and from this spirituality derives its sense of mission. In regard to the latter, while pentecostalism proper is debating the place of spirituality and theology in regard to pentecostal identity, Pentecostal orthodoxy sees striking commonalties (modalities of prayer, experiential spirituality, and so on) with the mystical theology of the Greek fathers and assumes such a spirituality, which inextricably combines personal experience of the divine with Christian dogma. I will discuss this subject at greater length in the next chapter. Both historic movements, monasticism and mysticism, are used within a Pentecostal orthodoxy as models for practicing a modern pentecostal spirituality. Thus, it can be said that the expression (along with other segments of pentecostalism) loses its exclusive hold on theological distinctives in light of being considered within the vein of historic Christianity before the Azusa Street revival of 1906.

The recovery of language, vestments, and knowledge about the early church by pentecostals does not in itself constitute a Pentecostal orthodoxy. Rather, the main demarcation of Pentecostal orthodoxy is made evident in the consistent liturgical and sacramental practices of its eucharistic communities.

Purpose. The overall purpose of a Pentecostal orthodoxy is to first situate pentecostal spirituality historically, away from a timeline originating solely in 1906. Second, it is to strengthen pentecostal spirituality and theology by recovering elements of classical Christianity that can provide a deeper understanding of both current and future practices and beliefs within pentecostalism as a whole. Last, given Pentecostalism's rapid global growth, a Pentecostal orthodoxy can have the ability to continue to spread its spirituality as well as aid in the spread of historical orthodoxy.

Gifts. Because a Pentecostal orthodoxy lends itself to a robust solidarity with the historic Christian mystical and monastic traditions, there are a number of gifts it both extends and enjoys. First, by way of contrast and comparison with the mystical and monastic traditions, pentecostalism as a whole (but a Pentecostal orthodoxy in particular) has access to a wide array of theological and spiritual treasures. Further, not only do such treasures provide pentecostalism an invigorating perspective toward its own future, but they also place the responsibility (along with other Christian traditions) of handing on orthodoxy in pentecostalism's lap. Given the incredible and rapid growth of global Pentecostalism, a Pentecostal orthodoxy will be a vital segment of pentecostalism in the coming decades, particularly in the Global South. Last, the expression opens the path toward a new way of having ecumenical dialogues and relationships, especially between pentecostals and Orthodox Christians.

Limits. Aside from this book, to my knowledge, there currently exists no major work that explores and examines the depth of a pentecostal orthodox spirituality. The movement itself is in its embryonic stage and needs both good scholarship and good practical ecclesial representation. Thus, it is to this endeavor I give myself in this work.

2

CAN ANYTHING ORTHODOX COME FROM PENTECOSTALISM?

BECAUSE THIS BOOK ULTIMATELY seeks a way of being pentecostal in the world in a way that is distinct and yet connected to both the broader Pentecostal movement and the various antecedent expressions of paleo-orthodoxy, a certain level of intrigue, skepticism, and criticism is expected. Over the years, since becoming public with my development of a Pentecostal orthodoxy, I have run into what I have deemed to be the Nathanaels of the world—believers from various Christian traditions who question whether anything orthodox can come from pentecostalism. These Nathanaels have manifested themselves at conferences, religious revivals, and yes, on social media. Indeed, it is not a strange thing for someone from another tradition who finds a social media post of mine concerning pentecostalism and the Great Tradition to question whether pentecostals can rightly recover "what they did not have."

These questions, however, usually stem from pentecostalism's conflicted and arduous quest toward becoming a global Christian tradition recognized as such by other Christian traditions. At present, pentecostalism, although a continually contested religious idea, is a global movement, with some forecasters projecting over a billion pentecostal believers before the year 2050.[1] Developmental changes in pentecostal theology and practice

---

[1] Philip Jenkins quotes David Barrett's *World Christian Encyclopedia* and Teresa Watanabe, "Global Convention Testifies to Pentecostalism's Revival," *Los Angeles Times*, May 31, 2001. See Jenkins, *The*

have been the product of integration and engagement with various twenty-first-century social, religious, theological, scientific, and educational developments in conjunction with ecumenical relations. Yet, there are still Nathanaels who will continue to consider pentecostalism a static twentieth-century religious sociological movement, given over to bouts of undefined and baseless enthusiasm, devoid of elements of historical Christianity. This type of thinking, however, has not been paying attention and has yet to consider the significant theological shifts undergone by segments of North American pentecostalism over the last five decades. With this in mind, let me attempt to contextually qualify my designation for the Nathanaels of the world.

The setting is Galilee, a mountainous northern region of Israel where Jesus will one day walk on water and challenge Simon Peter to do the same. This day, Jesus finds Philip of Bethsaida and instructs Philip to follow him. Philip instead goes and, finding Nathanael, declares, "We have found Him of whom Moses in the law, and also the prophets, wrote—Jesus of Nazareth, the son of Joseph" (Jn 1:45). Nathanael, upon hearing Philip's declaration, responds, "Can anything good come out of Nazareth?" (Jn 1:46).

Unlike the bustling urban and metropolitan areas, which boasted much commerce, education, and political exuberance, Nazareth at the time of Jesus was a rural farming area. Interestingly, however, Nazareth is believed to have had several failed political revolts against the Roman Empire.[2] This and other socioeconomic and educational factors are likely why Nathanael responds to Philip with such skepticism. Another factor is that the word *Nazareth* in Hebrew comes from the word *netser*, which means "branch" or "shoot," generally speaking of something coming out of, something that is of the same thing, as in a stump growing from a tree that has been chopped down.[3] The stump, then, would be called the "shoot" or the

---

Next Christendom: The Coming of Global Christianity (New York: Oxford University Press, 2002), 9. On pentecostalism as a contested religious idea, see Amos Yong, *The Spirit Poured Out on All Flesh: Pentecostalism and the Possibility of Global Theology* (Grand Rapids, MI: Baker Academic, 2005), 18.

[2] Paul Anderson, "Can Any Good Thing Come from Nazareth? The Hometown of Jesus," *HuffPost*, March 22, 2017, www.huffpost.com/entry/can-any-good-thing-come-from-nazareth-the-hometown_b_58d1f758e4b062043ad4ae1a.

[3] Marvin R. Vincent, *Word Studies in the New Testament* (New York: Scribner, 1887), 74.

netser. From a religious perspective, Philip's announcement to Nathanael would have reminded Nathanael of Isaiah's prophecy concerning a branch that would grow from out of the roots of the stem of Jesse (Is 11:1-5). Hearing Philip's declaration, Nathanael must have been confused as to how the promise of a savior could come from such a socially impoverished geographical location.

A neo- or independent pentecostalism that recovers the Great Tradition (i.e., Pentecostal orthodoxy) is best understood when framed as a movement or branch that comes out of the stumped tree that is classical Pentecostalism and thus displays a more rooted catholicity.[4] Here one could refer to what Amos Yong refers to when he speaks of many "Pentecostalisms," meaning a pentecostalism (lowercase *p*) within a Pentecostalism (uppercase *P*).[5] This distinction is usually made in order to distinguish between independent pentecostal ecclesial organizations (in this case those recovering the Great Tradition) and classical Pentecostal denominations, which stem from the revival of 1906. Given, however, that there also exists a small segment within classical Pentecostalism that looks to recover elements of the Great Tradition, the distinction between the two has more to do with an intentional conscious recognition of a spirituality situated within the broader historic Christian tradition, inclusive of the recovery of its classical exegetical and sacramental/liturgical elements. Thus the Nathanaels are those in either the historical liturgical/sacramental or Pentecostal camp who question whether anything orthodox can come from pentecostalism.

Before we venture to answer the Nathanaels' question, we have to ask a couple of preliminary questions of our own. First, what is a Pentecostal

---

[4]Pentecostalism can also be seen historically as the revivalist branch of Christendom that comes out of the stumped tree that is mainline Christianity. Those looking to explore this idea would benefit from Harvey Cox, *Fire from Heaven: The Rise of Pentecostal Spirituality and the Reshaping of Religion in the Twenty-First Century* (Cambridge, MA: Da Capo Press, 1995); Vinson Synan, *The Holiness Pentecostal Tradition: Charismatic Movements in the Twentieth Century* (Grand Rapids, MI: Eerdmans, 1997); and Douglas Jacobsen, *The World's Christians: Who They Are, Where They Are, and How They Got There* (Malden, MA: Wiley-Blackwell, 2011).

[5]Amos Yong utilizes the term *Pentecostalisms* when speaking of the *New International Dictionary of Pentecostal and Charismatic Movements* definition of the three kinds of Pentecostalism. See Yong, *Spirit Poured Out*, 18.

orthodoxy? What particular claims does it make, and what are its preliminary signs? While there can be numerous developing areas to which one
could point in order to explore the questions above, this chapter will briefly
examine

1. how a Pentecostal orthodoxy as the recovery of the Great Tradition
   by pentecostals must be done through a pentecostal framework that
   holds in tension modern pentecostal spirituality with a classical consensual sacramentality;

2. how a Pentecostal orthodoxy expresses, among other things, a continual commitment to the development of an experiential pentecostal
   spirituality that is educational and historical before a pentecostal theology (dogma) that is solely distinctive and exclusive;

3. how a Pentecostal orthodoxy is willing to reexamine its exclusive
   hold on certain spiritual distinctives and commits itself to redevel-
   oping a modern pentecostal spirituality seen in continuity with
   other Christian traditions; and

4. how, upon reexamining its exclusive hold on spiritual distinctives, a
   Pentecostal orthodoxy that recovers the Great Tradition intentionally and specifically situates itself within the broader Christian
   monastic and mystical traditions.

A PENTECOSTAL SPIRITUAL AND EDUCATIONAL FRAMEWORK

To be clear, if pentecostals are recovering the spirituality and theology of
the Great Tradition in interplay with a modern pentecostal framework,
then in essence they are developing a Pentecostal orthodoxy. Nowhere is
this fact displayed more poignantly than in the expression's beliefs and
practices regarding the sacraments of the church. As part of the broader
paleo-orthodox movement, Pentecostal orthodoxy continues to uphold
the commitment to a sacramental spirituality as expressed in its antecedent
expressions (evangelical orthodoxy, convergence, ancient-future faith).
The question we must ask ourselves now is, How do the belief and practices
of a sacramental spirituality within a Pentecostal orthodoxy differ from
pentecostalism's perspective as a whole?

I am often challenged by nonsacramental churches to show how they themselves are not sacramental even though the language of sacraments appears within their historical, liturgical, or organizational documents. "This church believes in sacraments," I am often told. "It's in the constitution." To which I respond that, away from regular practice and proper belief and understanding of the sacraments, there can be no true identification with them. We must remember, as Walter Hollenweger states, "There is no fully developed Eucharistic doctrine in the Pentecostal movement."[6] Therefore, let me say at the outset that my objective is not to attempt to develop a particular pentecostal sacramental theology, even though I believe that one is desperately needed. Rather, I argue that presently a Pentecostal orthodoxy looks to contribute to the subject by pointing out the distinct perspective between what modern pentecostal scholarship presents regarding the matter and what pentecostals recovering the great tradition are developing within their own sacramental spirituality.

Anyone looking to explore the mosaic of pentecostal perspectives concerning the sacraments has merely to consider Chris Green's superb treatment of the subject. Green presents possibly the first extensive look at how pentecostal scholarship has historically approached the subject of the sacraments. He brings together both early modern and postmodern pentecostal scholarship concerning sacramentality and the Lord's Supper, ultimately arguing that although pentecostals themselves have always held an inherent sacramental worldview, "there appears to have been in the last decade what can rightly be called a 'turn' to the sacraments among Pentecostals."[7] Signs of such a turn in Green's work include the acceptance and usage of the term *sacraments* over *ordinances*, the adoption somewhat of a belief in "real presence" at the Eucharist, and an eschatological understanding of the Eucharist as rehearsal for the supper of the Lamb.[8]

---

[6] Walter J. Hollenweger, *The Pentecostals: The Charismatic Movement in the Churches* (Minneapolis: Augsburg, 1972), 385.

[7] Chris E. W. Green, *Toward a Pentecostal Theology of the Lord's Supper: Foretasting the Kingdom* (Cleveland, TN: CPT, 2012), 71.

[8] See Daniel Tomberlin, *Pentecostal Sacraments: Encountering God at the Altar* (Cleveland, TN: Center for Pentecostal Leadership and Care, 2010), xi; Yong, *Spirit Poured Out*, 163; Simon Chan, *Liturgical Theology: The Church as a Worshiping Community* (Downers Grove, IL: IVP Academic, 2006), 71.

Green himself, however, acknowledges that this turn has taken two directions, with one group of pentecostal scholars looking to be informed by the broader Christian tradition while another group concentrates on developing a unique and authentic "Pentecostal account of the sacraments."[9] Joseph Lee Dutko also notes this. While Green sees two different directions, Dutko speaks of two streams of thought, with "the minority position that had a fairly positive view of the sacraments, and the majority position that downplayed any sacramental significance in the Lord's Supper or ignored the practice altogether." In Dutko's perspective, "in the end, the majority won out."[10]

Although pentecostalism has used the term *sacraments* as far back as the early 1900s, this does not mean that it has fully adopted the notion of there being seven sacraments or has fully believed in either a sacramental ontology or a sacramental causality (beliefs I define below). Further, as I have already mentioned, many pentecostal organizations that use the term *sacrament* in their organizational or catechetical documents only mean to identify baptism and the Lord's Supper. Here pentecostals seem to have more in common with the Eastern Orthodox tradition than with Roman Catholicism in that not only does the number of sacraments hold no particular dogmatic significance but the very notion of or belief in sacramentals and their usage (i.e., blessed or sacred objects) is similar.[11] Kallistos Ware attests to the same when, in speaking of the Eastern Orthodox Church's teaching on the number of sacraments, he states, "Only in the seventeenth century when the Latin influence was at its height, did this list become fixed and definite. Before that date Orthodox writers vary considerably as to the number of sacraments. . . . Even today the number seven has no particular dogmatic significance for Orthodox theology, but is used primarily as a convenience of teaching."[12] For Ware, those who would

---

[9]Green, *Toward a Pentecostal Theology*, 72.

[10]Joseph Lee Dutko, "Beyond Ordinance: Pentecostals and a Sacramental Understanding of the Lord's Supper," *Journal of Pentecostal Theology* 26 (2017): 257.

[11]Edith M. Humphrey, "Sacrifice and Sacrament: Sacramental Implications of the Death of Christ," in *The Oxford Handbook of Sacramental Theology*, ed. Hans Boersma and Matthew Levering (New York: Oxford University Press, 2015), 71.

[12]Timothy Kallistos Ware, *The Orthodox Church*, 3rd ed. (London: Penguin Books, 2015), 275.

speak strictly of there being seven sacraments must guard themselves against the misconception that there is not a hierarchy of sacramental pre-eminence. They also must guard against an isolationist notion that only relegates a sacramental character to the seven sacraments, away from other actions and objects that may indeed also possess such said sacramental character and be called sacramentals.[13]

As mentioned above, the use of the term *sacraments* by much of pente-costalism seems to be devoid of a sacramental ontology, which, according to Hans Boersma and Edith Humphrey, is an understanding of reality of the sacraments as participating in the very physical world they signify or point to.[14] Rather than keeping to a sacramental physical causality (convening or causes of grace), pentecostals seem to view sacraments through the lens of a sacramental occasionalism. According to Thomas White, this is the view that

> God alone is the author of grace in every sacramental action while the visible aspects of the rite are merely external signs of the invisible grace that is given. The pouring of water and pronouncement of the baptismal formula, for instance, are the occasion for the giving of grace, and God has assured the giving of grace whenever this solemn rite is correctly per-formed. In this case, the physical action of the sacrament is not a true effi-cient cause of grace, but only the mere occasion for that action on the part of God.[15]

A sacramental occasionalism as believed and practiced by most pente-costals does not hold that the sacramental action or rite itself causes regen-eration or grace, and therefore pentecostals have no need of (and most probably disagree with) the teaching of *ex opera operato* (by the very working of the sacrament). Instead, it seems as though the language of sacraments has been adopted in pentecostal organizational, historical, and liturgical documentation solely as a way of acknowledging the grace of

---

[13]Ware, *Orthodox Church*, 276.

[14]Hans Boersma, *Heavenly Participation: The Weaving of a Sacramental Tapestry* (Grand Rapids, MI: Eerdmans, 2011), 21-26. See also Edith M. Humphrey, "Sacrifice and Sacrament," 69.

[15]Thomas J. White, OP, "Sacraments and Philosophy," in Boersma and Levering, *Oxford Handbook of Sacramental Theology*, 583-84.

God, remembered at the time when the sacrament is celebrated. This is made even more evident by the fact that pentecostalism as a whole has no developed, organized, or central eucharistic liturgy.

As both a religious educator and a Pentecostal orthodox minister, I see the practice of a sacramental spirituality differently from some of my pentecostal colleagues. Therefore, I will attempt to lay out what distinctions I believe exist between some of the thinking explored above and to examine some of the key aspects and contributions made by a Pentecostal orthodoxy to the overall pentecostal sacramental conversation.

It must be stated and restated that segments of pentecostalism recovering the Great Tradition are opposed to the common idea that if one were to recover the liturgical/sacramental and theological elements of the Great Tradition, one would have to "come home" to one of the canonical churches (Roman Catholic, Eastern Orthodox, Anglican). In considering Green's analysis of how postmodern pentecostal scholarship's turn toward the sacraments "has moved in one or another of two directions,"[16] two things immediately come to mind.

For adherents to Pentecostal orthodoxy, Green's analysis regarding the direction of pentecostal scholarship toward the sacraments actually represents a dialectical and dynamic path with two steps. Most pentecostal scholars, according to Green, either "emphasized the need for Pentecostals to learn from the sacramental theology of the of the wider Christian tradition" or "are concerned primarily with developing a uniquely and authentically Pentecostal account of the sacraments."[17] A Pentecostal orthodoxy, in losing its exclusive hold on elements of pentecostal spirituality, looks first to recover and solidify a sacramental spirituality from within the classical Christian tradition (orthodoxy) and then, second, looks within its own pentecostal framework to develop a contextual account of the sacraments. This process is not a strict, linear move back toward the early church but a dynamic move that considers present context, goes back, and returns in order to develop within a pentecostal framework. The process is dialectical and resembles Joe Holland and Peter Henriot's

---

[16]Green, *Toward a Pentecostal Theology*, 71.
[17]Green, *Toward a Pentecostal Theology*, 71-72.

Pastoral Circle, which speaks of immersion, analysis, reflection, and response in regards to engagement with issues of faith and justice.[18] Considering this process as a two-step one of recovery from without and contextual development from within, rather than seeing them as two different groups, could develop a pedagogical pentecostal methodology that could unite us all around a similar epistemological theme. Let us consider these two steps more fully.

In lieu of holding exclusively to aspects of teaching concerning the Holy Spirit, a Pentecostal orthodoxy is willing to reexamine such exclusive holds in order to better situate itself within the broader Christian spiritual traditions (monastic and mystical). This statement might conjure up suspicion on the part of some pentecostals who have forgotten the distinctions between a modern Pentecostal movement, applicable to some, and historic pentecostal spirituality, inclusive of all. Here again, one needs to consider the wisdom of Steven Land. Land, in speaking of pentecostalism's need for a "re-visioning," states,

> The Pentecostal movement is in a period of theological adolescence. Tempted to forget or selectively remember the past, dangerously accommodated to North American middle- and upper-class culture, and having its supposedly distinctive experience, the baptism in the Spirit, marketed in every church or induced for the bored and impatient, Pentecostals are being asked to choose whom they will be. It is neither possible nor desirable merely to repeat the past, and pragmatism soon leads to cynical detachment and withdrawal. . . . Those who share this concern are convinced that Pentecostalism is more than a feeling, more than an episode in church or individual history, more than an added option for Christians whose personality profile happens to match. They see a second naivete, and a rekindling of the apocalyptical vision—expanded so as not to be so individualistic—of the kingdom of God. Along with Roman Catholics, Eastern Orthodox, and Protestants, Pentecostals too are being called to a renewed vision which addresses global and local pastoral issues.[19]

---

[18]Joe Holland and Peter Henriot, SJ, *Social Analysis: Linking Faith and Justice* (Ossining, NY: Center for Concern and Orbis Books, 1983).

[19]Steven J. Land, *Pentecostal Spirituality: A Passion for the Kingdom* (Cleveland, TN: CPT, 2010), 190-91.

"Revival" does not necessarily equal "new-vival," and perhaps we should
follow Saint Vincent's exhortation *dicas nove non dicas nova* (speak newly,
but do not speak new things).[20] Perhaps what we pentecostals have been
awaiting is a movement within our ranks in which holding loosely, if at all,
to our supposed distinctive experience opens us to levels of historic recovery in interplay with the power of the Spirit. Perhaps it is time for classical Pentecostalism to not only recover the whole of the Great Tradition
but to also reexamine its theological distinctives of separability, subse-
quence, and the role of grace within spiritual experience. In so doing, pentecostalism might be able to better convince traditions such as Eastern
Orthodoxy that elements of pentecostal spirituality such as glossolalia and
the overall concept of a continuationsim as it relates to gifts of the Spirit
are in continuation with the Great Tradition itself, bringing about greater
ecumenical understanding.

While most modern and postmodern pentecostal scholars use Protestant post-Reformational, neo-orthodox writings to develop and
substantiate their biblical-sacramental perspectives, those within a Pentecostal orthodoxy view sacramentality mainly through the "hermeneutical proximity" of the early fathers. Standing within their Wesleyan
Holiness heritage, Pentecostal orthodox adherents continue to hold to
John Wesley's last hermeneutical principle: "the historical experience of
the church, though fallible, is the better judge overall of Scripture's
meanings than later interpreters are likely to be, especially on their own."[21]
To this end, Christopher Hall writes that "the fathers are more proximate
beneficiaries of the apostolic traditions. . . . The fathers lived and worked
in hermeneutical proximity to the biblical writers, especially those of the
New Testament."[22]

Further, those within a Pentecostal orthodoxy not only recover the
writings of the earliest exegetes but, as part of the broader paleo-orthodoxy communitarian theological movement, also utilize Saint

---

[20]Vincent of Lérins, *Comminitotirum* 22.7.
[21]Albert C. Outler, *John Wesley's Sermons: An Introduction* (Nashville: Abingdon, 1991), 67.
[22]Christopher A. Hall, *Reading Scripture with the Church Fathers* (Downers Grove, IL: InterVarsity
   Press, 1998), 54.

Vincent of Lérins's commonitorium (*quod ubique, quod semper, quod ab omnibus creditum est*—everywhere, always, and by all) as their extracanonical normative interpretive arbiter.[23] Thomas Guarino, in commenting on Vincent's commonitorium, sees the same two-step concern for assuring orthodoxy and its vital progression, which resembles both of the concerns expressed by pentecostal scholars. Guarino suggests, "Vincent's major contemporary contribution is to be found in his attempt to understand how church teaching advances over time under the light of the Spirit and, relatedly, how the entire body of Christ is involved in the twin task of preserving the Christian faith and discerning its authentic progression."[24]

Oden, summarizing the ancient ecumenical method of scriptural discernment "everywhere, always, and by all" (i.e., universality, apostolic antiquity, and conciliar consent), suggests,

> The direction and momentum of orthodox interpretation are guided by a process of fair-minded historical inquiry, aided by the Holy Spirit, into what has been believed in all cultures where faith has been lived out, and believed from the beginning of the apostolic witness, and believed by general lay consent in the whole church over the whole world in all generations.[25]

Adherents of a Pentecostal orthodoxy are not against modern scholarship regarding sacramental spirituality. In fact, this type of spirituality is held in high esteem inasmuch as it stays within the confines of historical orthodox teaching. Here, in regard to questions concerning the incarnation, real presence, and the indwelling of the Word in the Eucharist, we rather look to Irenaeus, Ignatius of Antioch, Justin Martyr, and Gregory of Nyssa. Regarding the notion of an invocation of the Holy Spirit (epiclesis), we look to writers such as John Chrysostom, Ephraim of Syria, and Cyril of Jerusalem. We recognize the seven sacraments of the church and look to practice all seven, holding to a physical sacramental causality yet, as with

---

[23]See Thomas C. Oden, *The Rebirth of Orthodoxy: Signs of New Life in Christianity* (New York: Harper-Collins, 2003), 156-86; John C. Peckham, *Canonical Theology: The Biblical Canon, Sola Scriptura, and Theological Method* (Grand Rapids, MI: Eerdmans, 2016), 95-98.

[24]Thomas G. Guarino, *Vincent of Lérins and the Development of Christian Doctrine* (Grand Rapids, MI: Baker Academic, 2013), xxi.

[25]Oden, *Rebirth of Orthodoxy*, 162.

the Orthodox Church, recognize that the earliest Christian writers before
the 1700s never settled on a definite number.[26]

Concerning the Eucharist, we do not hold to the notion of transubstantiation as expressed by the Roman Catholic Church, although we
understand its Aristotelian underpinnings. Neither do we look to a pan-
sacramentality that ends in a quasi-Lutheran understanding of consub-
stantiation.[27] Rather, we speak, as already mentioned above, of a
participation in a "sacramental ontology" that presupposes a difference
between mere sign or symbol and a sacrament—the former having no
connection to thing it symbolizes, while the latter participates in the reality to which it points as a mystery.[28] In this, Pentecostal orthodoxy
agrees more with an Orthodox sacramental theology than with a Catholic
theology.[29] Last, in regard to the role of *ex opere operato* in the sacraments,
a theme majorly treated within the Donatist controversy, we do not
object, if and when the work done continues to be seen mainly through
a pneumatological lens.

After dialectically recovering an orthodox understanding of the sacraments, adherents of a Pentecostal orthodoxy pivot inward to develop a
pentecostal sacramentality using a pentecostal framework. In the case of
pentecostals recovering the Great Tradition, the structure of ideas or concepts about religion, the world, and the church (sacramentalism, liturgy,
and so on) stem from within pentecostalism as a second step in amalgamation with classical Christianity.

Developing a pentecostal framework is similar to developing what
James K. A. Smith calls a "pentecostal philosophy." For Smith, a pentecostal philosophy is not the articulation of a new kind of philosophy that
is sectarian in nature; rather, it is a pentecostal contribution to Christian
philosophy. In advocating for the task of a pentecostal philosophy Smith

---

[26]See Ware, *Orthodox Church*, 275; Constatine N. Tsirpanlis, *Introduction to Eastern Patristic Thought and Orthodox Theology*, Theology and Life Series (Collegeville, MN: Michael Glazier, 1990), 106.

[27]*Pan-sacramentality* is used by Andrew Davison to describe the idea that if all is holy, there is no need for distinction within the sacramental elements. See Davison, *Why Sacraments?* (London: SPCK, 2013), 9.

[28]Boersma, *Heavenly Participation*, 23.

[29]Boersma uses Alexander Schmemann, *For the Life of the World: Sacraments and Orthodoxy* (Crest-wood, NY: St. Vladimir's Seminary Press, 1997), 34-36, 68, 135-51.

means a pentecostal "social imaginary" that looks to articulate a worldview through the implicit practice of a pentecostal spirituality.[30] This is akin to how a Pentecostal orthodoxy argues for a recovery of the Great Tradition from within its own spirituality, which it understands as being in continuity with other traditions, rather than believing a recovery of the Great Tradition must lead one to "come home" to one of the canonical churches.

Although there are many good examples of some type of sacramental work being done within a pentecostal framework (as Green's work has shown), possibly the best example is Frank Macchia's "Tongues as a Sacramental Sign: Toward a Sacramental Understanding of Pentecostal Experience." Macchia, a classical Pentecostal theologian, sees an interplay between glossolalia as an initial and integral experience of the baptism of the Holy Spirit and a Roman Catholic and Reformed understanding of a sacramental sign. Macchia argues: "Glossolalia is a different kind of 'sacrament' than that which is conveyed in formalized and structured liturgies. Glossolalia accents the free, dramatic, and unpredictable move of the Spirit of God, while the liturgical traditions stress an ordered and predictable encounter with the Spirit." For Macchia, an experience of the Holy Spirit (*epektasis*) accompanied with tongues holds in tension "a visible audible human response that signifies the divine presence in the sense of actually participating in making it present." Within this thinking, glossolalia as evidence "is not rationalist evidence as much as a sacramental sign."[31]

Macchia's developmental theory of tongues as a sacramental sign within a pentecostal framework is both stimulating and creative. His thinking regarding tongues as a sacramental that both signifies and participates resembles C. S. Lewis's distinction between words on paper and normal speech, which only exists for the eye and the ear, and a picture, which participates in and is part of the visible world.[32] Macchia's openness to

---

[30]James K. A. Smith, *Thinking in Tongues: Pentecostal Contributions to Christian Philosophy* (Grand Rapids, MI: Eerdmans, 2010), xviii.

[31]Frank D. Macchia, "Tongues as a Sign: Toward a Sacramental Understanding of Pentecostal Experience," *Pneuma, the Journal of the Society for Pentecostal Studies* 15, no. 1 (1993): 63-64, 70.

[32]C. S. Lewis, *Transposition and Other Addresses* (London: Geoffrey Bles, 1949), 102.

reexamine the depth of sacramental limits is shared by diverse scholars, including Orthodox Bishop Kallistos Ware, who notes, "When we talk of seven sacraments, we must never isolate these seven from the many other actions in the Church which also possess a sacramental character, and which are conveniently termed sacramentals."[33]

Such an interplay, although creative and bold, does bring up several questions. For example, what sacramental configuration can be given to segments of pentecostalism that do not share a classical view of tongues as evidence of the baptism of the Holy Spirit? Further, since Macchia uses Catholic-Reformed sacramental thinking, is there any conversation surrounding a sacramental character of glossolalia as indelible? What impact would the Greek fathers' understanding of the soul-body correspondence have on pentecostalim's spirit-body correspondence in relation to tongues as a sacramental? Finally, what type of development could be constructed for glossolalia as a sacramental if, instead of utilizing Acts 2 in conjunction with a Catholic-Reformed understanding of sign and sacrament, we used the writings of Paul in 1 Corinthians 14 in conjunction with an Eastern Orthodox understanding of mystagogy, which does not distinguish between symbol and sacramental?[34]

SPIRITUALITY AND NOT JUST THEOLOGY

We must remember that "a pentecostal worldview is not a set of doctrines or dogmas. Instead, latent, implicit theological and philosophical intuitions are embedded within, and enacted by, pentecostal rituals and practice."[35] According to Land, these beliefs and practices are integrated "in the affections which are themselves evoked and expressed by those beliefs."[36] Therefore, in recovering the great tradition from a pentecostal framework, pentecostals themselves must be reminded of a classical truth: the essence of pentecostal identity is more rooted in its emphasis on

---

[33]Ware, *Orthodox Church*, 276.
[34]Schmemann, *For the Life of the World*, 135-51; Maximus the Confessor, *On the Ecclesiastical Mystagogy; A Theological Vision of the Liturgy by St. Maximus the Confessor*, ed. Jonathan J. Armstrong, Popular Patristic Series (Yonkers, NY: St. Vladimir's Seminary Press, 2019), chap. 23.
[35]Smith, *Thinking in Tongues*, xix.
[36]Land, *Pentecostal Spirituality*, 128.

spirituality than its dogmatic theology. Douglas Jacobsen, in echoing the same stance concerning pentecostal identity, states,

> Historically most pentecostals have said that identity comes first. They have said that it is the experience of the baptism of the Spirit (which requires only minimal instruction to recognize) that makes one a pentecostal believer. Understood in this sense, theology has nothing to do with becoming a pentecostal believer. Instead, pentecostal theology is something that comes later when a person begins to reflect more intentionally upon what he or she has experienced.[37]

A Pentecostal orthodoxy validates its recovery of orthodoxy through spiritual practice, not just through the recovery of theological doctrine. What makes sacramentality orthodox is not just its theologizing but ultimately its practice within our Pentecostal liturgy. Alexander Schmemann, in speaking of the tension between a sacramental theology and liturgy, writes, "In the early Church, in the writings of the Fathers, sacraments, inasmuch as they are given any systematic interpretation, are always explained in the context of their actual liturgical celebration, the explanation being, in fact, an exegesis of the liturgy itself in all its ritual complexity and concreteness."[38] It is interesting that Dutko, in dealing with Hollenweger's thinking concerning the centrality of the Lord's Supper in early pentecostal worship, suggests, "The problem is that this sacramental tradition was mostly in practice and not on paper."[39] It seems that the roles of practice and paper have been reversed. Might we be becoming great sacramental theologians but poor practitioners?

While a turn toward the sacraments may be evident within pentecostal scholarship, a major turn toward the same from within pentecostal congregations has yet to be seen. There are still many modern pentecostal believers whose spirituality seems to hold to a "Platonist-Christian synthesis" until it reaches the subject of the sacraments.[40] They revert back to a

---

[37]Douglas Jacobsen, *Thinking in the Spirit: Theologies of the Early Pentecostal Movement* (Bloomington: Indiana University Press, 2003), 9.

[38]Schmemann, *For the Life of the World*, 137.

[39]Dutko, "Beyond Ordinance," 258.

[40]"Platonist-Christian synthesis" is borrowed from Boersma, *Heavenly Participation*, 33.

suspicion-induced Catholo-phobia that calls for memorialism and negates the very spiritual and metaphysical beliefs they hold concerning anointing oil, handkerchiefs, laying on of hands, and speaking in tongues. Concerning sacramental practice, pentecostalism continues to hold a Zwinglian suspicion, while pentecostal scholarship overtheologizes, forgetting Friedrich Schleiermacher's warning that we must avoid the "over-intellectual bareness of the Zwinglian view."[41]

I myself came to recognize the real presence at the Lord's Supper not by examining propositional truths but by an experiential spirituality inclusive of a pneumatological and educational focus. Contrary to Dutko's statement concerning the absence of any mention of the Holy Spirit within pentecostal celebrations of the Lord's Supper, those of us practicing a weekly celebration of the sacrament of the Eucharist could never imagine a rite, rubric, or ritual without the Spirit's presence.[42] We also understand that celebrating the Eucharist often does not make us less pentecostal, any more than charismatic Catholics' baptism in the Holy Spirit makes them less Roman Catholic.[43] One can only wonder whether this type of fragmentation between a sacramental intellectualism and spirituality is part of what drove the Messalians to suggest that only a Eucharist where the Spirit was sensibly felt and recognized could be participated in.[44]

Because of a strong primitivistic-eschatological tension inherent within pentecostalism, the spirituality practiced in most pentecostal communities tends to be informed solely by the primitive church as described in the book of Acts. Thus their identity is commonly rooted in the same. Many adherents are generally uninformed of the historical presence of spiritual gifts and/or the affections within the first thousand years of the church's existence. Pentecostal spirituality, for the most part, begins with the primitive apostolic age, skips to the Azusa Street revival

---

[41] Friedrich Schleiermacher, *The Christian Faith*, 3rd ed. (New York: T&T Clark, 2016), 650.

[42] Dutko, "Beyond Ordinance," 261.

[43] See Kilian McDonnell and George T. Montague, *Christian Initiation and Baptism in the Holy Spirit: Evidence from the First Eight Centuries*, 2nd ed. (Collegeville, MN: Liturgical Press, 1994), 372-73.

[44] Columba Stewart, OSB, *Working the Earth of the Heart: The Messalian Controversy in History, Texts, and Languages to AD 431* (Oxford: Clarendon, 1991), 64.

of 1906, and lands in the present day with an orientation toward the eschatological coming of Christ.

Land, in addressing this distinctive, states,

> Pentecostals referred to themselves as an apostolic faith movement due to their desire to recover for the present age the faith and the power of the apostolic church. Paradoxically, it was this primitivistic, backward-looking concern with the early church which was responsible for their passion for the coming of Christ. For them, a restoration of primitive faith was a prelude to the restoration of all things.[45]

Land goes on to describe three kinds of existing pentecostal primitivism: ecclesiastical, ethical, and experiential. The first two were catalyzed by the last, directing all theoretical or theological foci existing in the first two kinds toward an openness to experiencing the second coming of Christ. Thus, believers were expected to evidence the same power, ecclesial structure, and holiness of apostolic New Testament Christians if they were to be "in eschatological continuity with the beginning and end of the church of Pentecost."[46]

The argument for validating such a selective understanding of ecclesial history, consistently made on the part of pentecostals, is that after the close of the New Testament, humanly made institutions, creeds, and traditions took over and diminished the Spirit's power and presence in the church. The Spirit's power, however, was supposedly returned to the church at Azusa and continues through a present pentecostal dispensation. The bias within pentecostal spirituality against creedal identity and historical apostolic traditions is one of the reasons pentecostals placed a singular emphasis on affective experientialism, many times negating key historical elements within spirituality considered orthodox. Thus, pentecostal identity is less informed by the wisdom and insight of two thousand years of church witness. Land, summarizing Lesslie Newbigin's understanding of pentecostalism's view on creedal identity, states that a concern for the Spirit's leading solely through "right affections" is

---

[45]Land, *Pentecostal Spirituality*, 51.
[46]Land, *Pentecostal Spirituality*, 51-52.

responsible for leading early Pentecostals to "disdain and eschew what they believed were man-made creeds." For Land, "It was not that they had no fundamental beliefs—their periodicals and testimonies make it obvious that they did—rather, the objections was to a creedalism which they believed brought disunity and rejected the new blessing that the sovereign Spirit was restoring among them."[47]

Land's statement is a reminder of Newbigin's omission of the qualifying term *orthodox* when referring to pentecostalism. One of the reasons Newbigin does not qualify pentecostalism as orthodox is precisely because pentecostals place the presence and work of the Spirit over creedal identity. Pentecostalism will not be able to develop a mature pentecostal theology or identity without a spirituality that is historically inclusive and educational. The question must be asked, then, How can a Pentecostal orthodoxy effectively express a continual commitment to the development of a pentecostal spirituality that is classical, consensual, and educational before a pentecostal theology (dogma) that is solely distinctive and exclusive? What does it mean to have a pentecostal spirituality that is educational, classical, and ultimately orthodox?

EDUCATIONAL AND HISTORICAL ORTHOPATHY

As a pentecostal religious educator and ministerial practitioner recovering the Great Tradition, I am constantly reminded of the educational nature of an experiential and affective pentecostal spirituality. Thus, I would be doing the Pentecostal orthodox expression a disservice and this work would not be complete if I did not include my brief religious-educational contribution to the conversation regarding a Pentecostal orthodox spirituality.

Methodist theologian Theodore Runyon, in studying John Wesley's focus on experientialism, coined the term *orthopathy* to describe how right affections fuse with right beliefs (orthodoxy) and right practices (orthopraxy) within Wesley's theological framework.[48] For Runyon, orthopathy is a religious experience, an event of knowing between the divine Source

---

[47]Land, *Pentecostal Spirituality*, 22.
[48]T. H. Runyon, "A New Look at Experience," *Drew Gateway* (Fall 1987): 44-55; Runyon, *The New Creation: John Wesley's Theology Today* (Nashville: Abingdon, 1998).

(God) and a human participant (believer), providing a necessary but currently missing complement to orthodoxy and orthopraxy.[49]

Dale Coulter, professor of historical theology at Pentecostal Theological Seminary, in describing how Runyon's work on the affections has been utilized by Wesleyan and pentecostal historians, speaks of the "connection between divine encounters and the process of Christian development."[50] Coulter's statement raises the question: How does pentecostal affectivity through divine encounter (orthopathy) influence Christian educational development, which can lead to right believing (orthodoxy)?[51]

Although the study of affections or orthopathy within the Christian tradition has primarily been done within the field of historical theology, the insights from such a review in interplay with an educational epistemology can bring pentecostalism to a recognition that there has not only been an abundance of pneumatological movement within the first two centuries of the Christian era but that this movement has also been in most ways catechetical. This is particularly true when one considers that even before the Christian tradition had an agreed-upon canon of Scriptures, worship was the primary agent of Christian formation into orthodoxy.

Orthodoxy can be defined as "right belief," in connection with a classical textual tradition (as seen in Oden).[52] However, it can also be defined as "true" or "straight teaching."[53] There exists, then, an underlying educational sense that when placed with a pentecostal affective spirituality as "right feeling" or orthopathy, orthodoxy can aid pentecostals recovering

---

[49]T. H. Runyon, "The Importance of Experience for Faith" (Minister's Week address, Emory University, Atlanta, GA, 1988).

[50]Dale M. Coulter introduction to *The Spirit the Affections and the Christian Tradition*, ed. Dale M. Coulter and Amos Yong (Notre Dame, IN: University of Notre Dame Press, 2016), 5.

[51]Because my current focus is more on how the affections can be educational, this work does not explore the various theological themes outlined by Coulter. However, Coulter's contributions to *The Spirit, the Affections, and the Christian Tradition*, along with those of other theological scholars, are a must-read for any pentecostal looking to both solidify and expand their understanding of the affections within the Great Tradition.

[52]"Orthodoxy," in *The Oxford Dictionary of the Christian Church*, ed. F. L. Cross and Elizabeth A. Livingstone (Oxford: Oxford University Press, 2005), 1206.

[53]"What Orthodox Christians Believe," Antiochian Orthodox Christian Diocese of North America, 2020, http://ww1.antiochian.org/whatorthodoxbelieve; "Orthodoxy," The Saint Constantine School, 2017, www.saintconstantine.org/about/orthodoxy.

the Great Tradition in developing a spirituality that is educational and ultimately orthodox. This type of pentecostal, educational spirituality in the present mirrors the great ancient saying of the church *lex orandi, lex credendi, lex vivendi* in that it looks to develop right affections through an experience of worship first (orthopathy), which leads to right belief or teaching (orthodoxy), ultimately leading to right action (orthopraxy).[54]

So then, how does pentecostal affectivity through divine encounter (orthopathy) influence Christian educational development, which can lead to right believing (orthodoxy)? Land states, "Orthodoxy (right praise-confession), orthopathy (right affections), and orthopraxy (right praxis) are related in a way analogous to the interrelation of the Holy Trinity." God creates humanity and endows them with a spirituality, which in Land's words "is at once cognitive, affective and behavioral, thus driving toward a unified epistemology, metaphysics, and ethics." For Land, "the personal integrating center of orthodoxy and orthopraxy is orthopathy, those distinctive affections which are belief shaped, praxis oriented, and characteristic of a person. Affections are neither episodic, feeling states, nor individualistic sentiments."[55] Affections or orthopathy within pentecostal spirituality, unlike everyday feelings, are composed of and determined by the biblical narratives, which evidence the marks of particular communal and historical location.[56] These affections represent a communal understanding of the worship seen in Acts 2 and Revelation 4. They are also integrative of the Spirit's leading, initiation, and sustaining, having as their objective God as the source and objective of all Christian affections.

Thus, now that I have reestablished that there exists an educational epistemology within an affective spirituality (orthopathy) that informs right believing (orthodoxy) and leads to right practice (orthopraxy), the question becomes, What educational models or frameworks can pentecostalism utilize?

The symbiotic relationship between orthopathy, orthodoxy, and orthopraxy as developed within the field of historical theology finds an ally in the

---

[54]*Lex orandi, lex credendi, lex vivendi* means "The church's worship informs, it believes, it lives."
[55]Land, *Pentecostal Spirituality*, 31, 34.
[56]Land, *Pentecostal Spirituality*, 34.

epistemological framework of experiential education. From an educational perspective, in discussing how a pentecostal experiential spirituality can be educative and ultimately orthodox, there are a number of wonderful works from top educators and theologians to turn to. These include the work of American philosopher William James, the seminal and innovative work of Maria Harris, and the crucial and contextual work of Cheryl Bridges Johns, which explores the intersection between pentecostal catechesis and Paulo Freire's educational philosophy. However, in an attempt to provide this work with an introductory educational framework akin to historical theology's alignment of right affections with right belief, I will consider the educational and experiential work of John Dewey and Gabriel Moran.

For Moran, "the keyword for beginning a description of education is interaction." *Interaction* is both subjective and objective in that it deals with how an organism and the various forms of life transform each other. Central to Moran's idea of education as interaction is the concept of a sense of "end," which according to Moran should be envisioned as purpose or meaning but not termination. On the one hand, educational interactions are not random. They are processes that have purpose and meaning. They aim to lead those involved out toward some end, some greater sense of understanding or insight. On the other hand, educational interactions should not terminate or come to an end. Rather, if they are to prepare people to engage in the continual unfolding of their lives and human history, they must be lifelong. Educational interactions have an end (meaning, purpose, design) but are without end (termination).[57]

Moran's description of education as the interaction of life forms with end and without end is reminiscent of John Dewey's experiential philosophy of education. First, Dewey envisions the aspects of education and experience as "the experiential continuum," meaning that an educational experience must be in continuity or connect with the significant knowledge of past experience. Second, within the experiential continuum there is also the principle of *interaction*. Interaction for Dewey "assigns equal rights to both factors in experience-objective and internal conditions. Any normal

---

[57] Gabriel M. Moran, *Showing How: The Act of Teaching* (New York: Continuum, 1997), 150, 156.

experience is an interplay of these two sets of conditions. Taken together, or in their interaction, they form what we call a situation."[58] Thus, while educational experiences must be in continuity with significant knowledge of the past, the present interaction involved in such experiences must modify and may even transform past knowledge. According to Dewey, experiences that are in continuity with the past and that involve meaningful interactions in the present are likely to prompt impulses within a person that can lead them toward the future. However, for these impulses to be transformed so that they have true educational value, they must be guided by proper intelligent observation, that is, reflection and organization of the subject matter experienced. In other words, genuine educational experiences lead a person to become more reflective and intelligent in learning from and then guiding life experiences.

From this perspective, a developing or maturing pentecostal spirituality that takes Moran and Dewey's educational work into account leads pentecostal believers who are recovering the Great Tradition in discerning and developing an educational spiritual framework that exhibits an experiential continuum through an interaction and connection with significant knowledge of a historical spirituality of the past. This interaction, as stated above, is dynamic and dialectical, and assigns both spiritual forms of pentecostal life equal rights to their experience-objective and internal conditions, creating an educational experience that has end (meaning) but is without end (termination). This type of spirituality can be aptly described as a pedagogy of the Spirit in that it exhibits the Holy Spirit's methodology of bringing right teaching (orthodoxy) to pentecostal believers through experiential interaction of the affections (orthopathy).

Here again Stanley Burgess's work on pentecostalism as a historic "people of the Spirit" comes to the forefront in that it defines and broadens pentecostalism as a spirituality and identity established before 1906. There exists, then, an ontological praxis within a modern pentecostal spirituality that looks to recover the Great Tradition that can rightly be defined as both educational and orthodox inasmuch as it allows itself to be informed by

---

[58]John Dewey, *Experience and Education* (New York: Touchstone Books, 1938), 33, 42.

the broader tradition both before and after 1906. Further studies regarding pentecostal spirituality and educational methodologies that aid both its spirituality and theology on its quest toward maturity are a must.

ASCETIC MONASTIC AND MYSTICAL TRADITION

While all expressions of the paleo-orthodox movement claim continuity with the Great Tradition, perhaps one of the most distinctive features of a Pentecostal orthodoxy is that, unlike its historical antecedents, it claims a specific continuity with the broader Christian monastic and mystical traditions.

The claim that pentecostalism lacks any kind of continuity with historic orthodoxy at worst exposes a bias and underdeveloped historical, spiritual, and theological framework. At best, it represents pentecostalism's inability to effectively discern its place historically and communicate the same to other Christian traditions. Often this kind of thinking has its roots both in the misunderstood and unexplained phenomenological experiences that occurred at Azusa and in the fanatic doctrines and actions of modern prosperity-gospel preachers who are quickly labeled Pentecostals. Father Alexis Trader, an Orthodox monk living in the Karakallou Monastery on Mount Athos, is an example of this type of thinking. Trader, in speaking of a Pentecostal discontinuity with orthodoxy, states,

> Although Pentecostals may try to show continuity with the past and how their movement predates the twentieth century by referring to a series of bizarre and highly questionable heretical sects from the Montanists and Gnostics to the Swiss Anabaptists, this new form of Christianity in fact began to be formed in the womb of some of the more unusual revival movements at the close of the nineteenth century and the threshold of the twentieth. It is a strange tale of well-meaning, but misguided seekers, who would begin with the reasonable, but often ended up with the ridiculous.[59]

Trader's answer to Pentecostalism's discontinuity and experiential naivete is easy—come home to the Orthodox Church. In telling of how a "large" evangelical group came to the Orthodox Church, he writes to Pentecostals

---

[59]Alexis Trader, *In Peace Let Us Pray to the Lord: An Orthodox Interpretation of the Gifts of the Spirit* (Protecting Veil, 2014), 128.

looking to be certain that their experience of the Holy Spirit is genuine: "Even as those former Evangelicals found a church far more scriptural than anything they formerly imagined, so Pentecostals would find a church much more laden with gifts, and especially the fruits of the Holy Spirit, than anything they could possibly conceive."[60]

Although well-meaning, I am sure, Trader's comments reveal the type of postmodern misplaced mockery to which pentecostalism is presently charged with responding. Trader's argument as well as his invitation must be challenged in light of the depth of historical, theological, and spiritual development undergone by pentecostalism, particularly within the last five decades. What segment of pentecostalism is Trader referring to when he makes his statement? This question is important considering that, in answer to thinking such as Trader's concerning Pentecostalism's reference to the Montanist movement, *The New International Dictionary of Pentecostal and Charismatic Movements* sets the record straight:

> Modern pentecostals who have identified with the Montanists have for-
> gotten that the founders of the New Prophecy were not Biblicist and that
> they were much more radically ascetic than 20th-century people of the
> Spirit. Perhaps it would be more useful to correlate the evolution of modern
> pentecostal groups to changes that occurred in Montanism over the course
> of its five centuries of existence.[61]

While there are some outside pentecostalism who, like Trader, attempt to discount pentecostalism's claims of continuity with the Christian past, and thus with orthodoxy, there are those within pentecostalism, such as Land and Coulter, whose research sees modern pentecostal spirituality sharing similarities with other Christian traditions, in particular with the mystical and monastic traditions.

Ascetic monasticism and pentecostalism. In speaking of modern pentecostalism's common ground with Christian asceticism and later

---

[60]Trader, *In Peace*, 19. Trader here is referring to evangelical orthodoxy and the group that went over to the Antiochians and the Orthodox Church of America. The group has been believed to be about 2000 people although exact figures have not been ascertained.

[61]S. M. Burgess, "Montanism," in *The New International Dictionary of Pentecostal and Charismatic Movements*, ed. Stanley M. Burgess and Eduard M. Van Der Mass (Grand Rapids, MI: Zondervan, 2002), 903-4.

monastic movements, various historical and spiritual similarities have been examined. For starters, each movement exhibited a historical-eschatological tension that led to a distancing from the politics of a state/imperial Christendom in lieu of preparing for the second coming of Christ. The apostle Paul's interpretation of Jesus' hard sayings concerning the kingdom of heaven and conventional values of the world constructed the platform for historic Christian asceticism. In the early third and fourth century, reacting to the identity of a newly legalized state church, Christians retreated into the deserts of Egypt and Syria. Here, "many who found the new ways of Christian life alien knew themselves called to continue to live an eschatological dimension that they could now only find outside the cities."[62] The movement into the desert along with Christian asceticism practiced by monastics, according to Constantine Tsirpanlis, was not only in response to the "progressive worldliness and corruption of the Church and State," but was also to "manifest its [monastic asceticism's] true spirit, and in the process, to provide an atmosphere in which monks could seek perfection through the ascetic life."[63]

There are a few voices worth noting within pentecostalism who highlight the similar historical-eschatological tension between the ascetic monastic movement and pentecostalism. Allan Anderson compares modern pentecostalism to monasticism, which he sees as a "charismatic movement that reacted to what seemed to be cold orthodoxy."[64] Amos Yong similarly believes that pentecostalism shares monasticism's retreat from the world in political and spiritual protest. Yong highlights the shared political distinctiveness between early monasticism and early Pentecostal perfectionism, which "can be seen in a different guise in the New Monasticism of the present time."[65] Both traditions, therefore, within their early spirituality, exhibited an affinity for a Christian eschatological/apocalyptic

---

[62]Benedicta Ward, ed. and trans., *The Desert Fathers: Sayings of the Early Christian Monks* (New York: Penguin Books, 2003), ix.

[63]Constantine N. Tsirpanlis, *Introduction to Eastern Patristic Thought and Orthodox Theology* (Collegeville, MN: Liturgical Press, 1991), 151.

[64]Allan Anderson, *An Introduction to Pentecostalism: Global Charismatic Christianity* (New York: Cambridge University Press, 2004), 19.

[65]Amos Yong, *In the Days of Caesar: Pentecostalism and Political Theology* (Grand Rapids, MI: Eerdmans, 2010), 192.

passion away from a dominant imperial or state-led Christianity. For Pentecostals in the early 1900s, theirs was an escape not into the desert but into weeklong revivals, tent meetings, and prayer meetings, which constituted a way of escape from mainline politics and religious consciousness as they awaited the second coming of Jesus. Land, in characterizing the same apocalyptic expectation within Pentecostal spirituality, states,

> This "promise-fulfillment, already-not yet" is a tensed dynamic which characterizes Christianity's eschatological passion. From time to time when the tension is resolved prematurely—either in the direction of an other-worldly, "not yet" escapism or a this worldly, "already" accommodation—there arise movements of restoration, revival, awakening, and renewal to remind the church that it is the eschatological mother whose sons and daughters are meant to prophesy. Pentecostalism was and is such a movement.[66]

Coulter has perhaps best captured the spiritual similarities between monasticism and pentecostalism. Coulter believes that "by rediscovering what they have in common with monasticism, pentecostals can begin to locate themselves within the larger tapestry of Christian tradition whose waters even now supply life and energy to the century-old movement." He goes on to link early monasticism with Pentecostal spirituality through what he describes as three common threads: (1) an emphasis on the spiritual life as warfare, (2) the need for conscious experiences of conversion that fuel a journey into ever-deepening degrees of relationship with God, and (3) the desire to bring reform and renewal to the larger Christian church.[67]

The effectiveness of Coulter's approach lies in that each thread presented is briefly treated by comparing the life and work of an early or medieval monastic figure with the life and work of a modern Pentecostal figure. An emphasis on the spiritual life as warfare, for example, is best demonstrated by Evagrius of Pontus, a fourth-century Christian monk and theologian, and by Pentecostals such as Elizabeth Sisson, a prominent evangelist, church planter, and author instrumental in the missional

---

[66]Land, *Pentecostal Spirituality*, 3.
[67]Dale Coulter, "Pentecostals and Monasticism: A Common Spirituality?," *Assemblies of God Heritage* 30 (2010): 43, www.yumpu.com/en/document/read/11969637/pentecostals-and-monasticism-flower -pentecostal-heritage-center.

development of the early Pentecostal movement. Both figures resemble the ascetic spiritual athlete (askesis), who sees spiritual warfare occurring in the battleground of the mind, which is the arena of struggle between the "divine, human and demonic wills."[68] For Evagrius, "All the demonic thoughts (*logismoi*) import concepts (*noemata*) of perceptible things into the soul and in this way the demons wage a veritable war against our human appetite." This battle can only be fought through prayer, fasting, and the reading of Scripture. Evagrius's understanding of how the demonic attacks the thoughts through the importation of concepts into the soul is similar to Sisson's testimony of her divine healing. Sisson recalls, "The enemy hissed into my soul, how I had failed God and got off his ground, else I would be healed or taking another tack, how God had failed me, and broken all His promises."[69]

Coulter's methodology of comparing and ultimately converging the teachings of early church figures with the spiritual experiences of modern pentecostals represents one of the ways in which pentecostal spirituality is recovering a historic orthodoxy. The shortening of the distance between the spirituality that has always existed within the church and the spirituality that was revived in North America in 1906 is accomplished by a critical historical analysis that is needed if pentecostalism is ever to be seen as a movement situated within the broader mystical and monastic Christian tradition.

Mystical tradition and pentecostalism. Although most pentecostal scholars have usually dealt with a pentecostal theology from a Catholic or Reformational perspective, a number of pentecostal scholars are beginning to show interest in the similarities between pentecostal spirituality and the mystical tradition.

In his phenomenal work *Pentecostalism as a Christian Mystical Tradition*, Daniel Castelo explores pentecostalism's philosophical and spiritual identity as a mystical tradition. His work calls for a theological

---

[68]Coulter, "Pentecostals and Monasticism," 45. See Joseph H. Lynch, "The Ascetic Movement," in *Early Christianity: A Brief History* (New York: Oxford University Press, 2010). Lynch suggests that the Greeks, who loved the competition, used the word *askesis* to refer to the training an athlete had to endure in order to gain victory.

[69]Coulter, "Pentecostals and Monasticism," 44.

method that takes into account pentecostalism's rejection of any division between its spirituality and theology, and further argues that by recovering both the language and ethos of Christian mysticism, pentecostalism develops a kind of "God-knowledge" that holds in tension intellect and spiritual engagement. In wrestling with the concept of the term *movement*, which is generally associated with pentecostalism, he sees instead that the connection between experiential spirituality and theology situates pentecostalism within the broader Christian tradition rightly known as mystical. His emphasis on pentecostalism as a mystical tradition comes through its "persistent, passionate, and widespread emphasis on encounter,"[70] which pulls it out from underneath evangelicalism and sets it on its own two feet.

Castelo's work is exhaustive and expansive, and it cannot be totally addressed here. His identification of pentecostalism as a mystical tradition does help to develop a firm epistemological foundation for segments of pentecostalism looking to better identify themselves with the recovery of the Great Tradition. This aim, however, cannot stand on its own unless pentecostalism itself it situated within the broader Christian mystical tradition, for, as Simon Chan writes, "When Pentecostals come to see their distinctives as part of the larger tradition . . . they can preserve them and maintain their integrity."[71]

If there is any weak point in Castelo's work, it is that he draws almost exclusively from medieval Latin (Catholic) mystics such as Teresa of Ávila and Saint John of the Cross to make his argument. Here again, it seems that pentecostals, for as much as they would like to disassociate themselves from the Roman Church, cannot do away with its mystics and theologians, a fact that is representative of a Western historical methodology inherited from evangelicalism. If pentecostals are looking for where the spirituality-theology divide could be lively and interactive, then I suggest we look intently at the mystical theology of the Greek Orthodox fathers.

---

[70]Daniel Castelo, *Pentecostalism as a Christian Mystical Tradition* (Grand Rapids, MI: Eerdmans, 2017), 37, 80.

[71]Simon Chan, *Pentecostal Theology and the Christian Spiritual Tradition* (Eugene, OR: Wipf & Stock, 2000), 7.

Land is perhaps one of the first and strongest advocates for a comparison between pentecostal experience and Orthodox mystical spirituality. In speaking of pentecostalism's continuity and discontinuity with other Christian streams, Land states, "It is more Eastern than Western in its understanding of spirituality as perfection and participation in the divine life (theosis). In this regard it has much to learn from persons like Gregory of Nyssa, Macarius the Egyptian, and St. Symeon the New Theologian. It is both ascetic and mystical."[72] Land's statement should be noted by pentecostals who agree with Castelo's presentation of pentecostalism as a mystical tradition. A close examination of the life, ministry, and writings of Macarius and Symeon would present pentecostals with a mystical spirituality much closer to modern pentecostal experience than Teresa of Ávila or John of the Cross. Investigations into Symeon's understanding of the "consciousness of grace" and his experiences of light, tears, and second baptism in the Spirit, along with Macarius's understanding of the soul-body correspondence over against pentecostalim's spirit-body correspondence, would have an enormous impact on pentecostalism as a mystical tradition.

If, as Castelo argues, pentecostalism can be rightly called a mystical tradition, it cannot do so without first being situated within the whole Christian mystical tradition (East and West). Further, it cannot do so without the inconvenience of self-reexamination. There and only there can pentecostalism, according to Kyle Smith, become "more than a description . . . [but] a vision for what Pentecostalism could be were it to fully claim its heritage."[73]

---

[72]Land, *Pentecostal Spirituality*, 18.

[73]Kyle Smith, "Author Meets Critics: Responding to Daniel Castelo's *Pentecostalism as a Christian Mystical Tradition,*" *Pneuma* 40, no. 4 (2018): 539.

3

PENTECOSTALS ON A
PENTECOSTAL TRAIL

In a conversation with a friend who is a priest in the Orthodox Church, I bemoaned how our segment of pentecostalism recovering the Great Tradition seemed to be neither pentecostal enough for pentecostals nor orthodox enough for the Orthodox. "We're stuck in the middle, I guess," I proclaimed with a sigh of discouragement.

No, he responded, "You're a bridge. That's why you're in the middle. That's what bridges do. They bring both worlds together."

I have often reflected on that particular conversation, amazed at the love, compassion, and understanding of my Orthodox friend. I wonder, Why did he not attempt to validate his own tradition by calling me to the Orthodox Church, as though that were the only way I was going to sense any type of validation? The fact is, however, he did not. Instead, he was able to hold in ecumenical tension his own ecclesial identity and at the same time recognize something that I could not at the moment—that there is value in being in between, expressing, to some extent, the best of both worlds.

During the Spirit-led charismatic renewal movement of the 1960s–1980s Roman Catholics and Anglicans, and to some extent even Orthodox Christians, remained within their respective traditions after having recovered or experienced the baptism of the Holy Spirit as well as charismatic gifts. Yet when I as a pentecostal believer recover or experience historic liturgical and sacramental spirituality through the same Spirit, I am told that I must go into one of the canonical churches.[1] Many of these same canonical churches today hold a vast amount of pentecostal converts who now rage against pentecostalism, proclaiming, often forcefully, that pente-costalism is a falsehood, a heresy, a sham!—and that pentecostals who truly want to recover the Great Tradition must "come home" to the true church.

This kind of thinking is reminiscent of Robert Webber's book *Evangel-icals on the Canterbury Trail*,[2] where he shares his own personal journey of the events that led him from being an ordained minister in the Reformed church into the Anglican tradition. Webber also shares the personal stories of a handful of other believers who also made a similar transition. The book itself, although full of insightful personal stories and information con-cerning the Great Tradition, makes its premise clear: in order to recover the Great Tradition, one must transition from one tradition (evangelical trail) to another (Canterbury Anglican trail). Similar suggestions have also been made by other former evangelicals who have gone into other historic traditions, such as Peter Gillquist and Thomas Howard.[3] Influenced by the writings of former evangelicals or pentecostals, there exists a way of thinking, both within and outside pentecostalism, that in order to truly recover and practice historic liturgy and sacramentality, one must leave one's present tradition or affiliation.

But again, is that what Roman Catholics, Anglicans, and the Orthodox did during the charismatic renewal? Was there a multitude of pentecostal voices who, after Catholics or Anglicans received the baptism of the Holy Spirit, were telling the same to come home into the pentecostal church or tradition? For that matter, did Webber truly have to transition from the

---

[1]Timothy B. Cremeens, *Marginalized Voices: A History of the Charismatic Movement in the Orthodox Church in North America 1972–1993* (Eugene, OR: Pickwick, 2018). Creemens speaks of the same conformist and nonconformist dispositions among Pentecostals, charismatics, and mainline de-nominations (39-47).

[2]Robert Webber and Lester Ruth, *Evangelicals on the Canterbury Trail: Why Evangelicals Are Attracted to the Liturgical Church* (New York: Morehouse, 2012).

[3]Peter Gillquist transitioned into the Orthodox Church and wrote *Becoming Orthodox: A Journey to the Ancient Christian Faith* (Chesterton, IN: Conciliar Press, 1989). See also Thomas Howard, *Evangelical is Not Enough: Worship of God in Liturgy and Sacrament* (San Francisco: Ignatius Press, 1984), and Thomas Howard, *On Being Catholic* (San Francisco: Ignatius Press, 1997), which describe his journey from evangelicalism into the Roman Catholic Church.

Reformed church to the Anglican Church in order to live out his spirituality within the Great Tradition? I do understand that there are some
liberties within some nondenominational churches, as well as some denominations, that do not extend to some of the confessional traditions, but
was there really no room for Webber to recover the Great Tradition within
the Reformed church? Unfortunately, the answer in Webber's case was no.
Yet his case is not emblematic of all cases—thus our conundrum. If pentecostals, in a similar manner to Webber, are on a trail toward recovering the
Great Tradition yet see no reason to transition to another tradition, but
rather see within their own tradition the opportunity and space for both
orthodox practice and belief, what do we name that trail?

Webber, in referencing his own journey into the recovery of the Great
Tradition, speaks of walking through what he calls the "three stages of faith,"
familial faith, searching faith, and owned faith.[4] It should be noted that
Thomas Oden experienced a crisis of faith similar to what Webber describes. For Webber, his crisis of faith was a wrestling with rationalistic
evangelicalism mixed with a yearning for a return to mystery mainly in
worship (a focus he links with his experience at St. Michael's Catholic
Church's vigil in 1972). For Oden, however, his crisis of faith was a wrestling with the theological mishaps of modernity and neo-orthodoxy. His
experience of revelation occurred within the context of the academy, which
led him toward the theology and exegesis of the early church fathers.

This initial experience of a crisis of spiritual faith, which many pentecostals
who are recovering the Great Tradition experience, seems to be mainly with
an evangelical rationalism. This wrestling is combined with a yearning for a
greater sense of mystery in worship, particularly the Eucharist. Ultimately,
however, after some time of practice, study, and formation, the same individuals end up also experiencing a crisis of faith with modern theological beliefs and, like Oden, yearn to know the Fathers and their writings more closely.

My own journey into the recovery of the Great Tradition is no less
similar to the situational challenges mentioned above. I, too, experienced
a crisis of faith, having to acknowledge each of Webber's stages of faith

---

[4]Robert Webber and Lester Ruth, *Evangelicals on the Canterbury Trail: Why Evangelicals Are Attracted to the Liturgical Church*, rev. ed. (New York: Morehouse, 2012), xv-xxi.

until coming to an owned embodied faith. Yet in order to better grasp my story, we must start at the very beginning.

MY STORY: A FAMILIAL FAITH

I was born in Rio Piedras, Puerto Rico. My family is from a place called Santurce, a municipality on the northeastern part of the Island that is one of Puerto Rico's most densely populated areas. When I was a year old, my entire family (including grandparents, uncles, and aunts) decided to move to Paterson, New Jersey, seeking a more stable environment for the family. In those days, both my mother and father worked in the Atlantic City casinos, my grandfather was hired to do construction, and my grandmother worked at a paper-making factory.

I am the oldest of eight children (three boys and five girls). My formative years as a child were spent with the first three of my sisters on trips to the lake, getting caught outside in rainstorms, candy, stickball, and playing in an open fire hydrant in the summer. I have many fond memories of my childhood, and even today when I hear a certain type of music or smell a certain scent, I am immediately transported back to the glory days of my youth.

I cannot tell you with certainty when my mother and father decided to come to Christ. Aside from being told about having Pentecostal roots back in Puerto Rico, the only other event I know of is my father's radical conversion experience, which occurred on one-drug infused night while he was working at the casino. The next thing I can remember I was sitting at the altar with my three sisters at the Pentecostal Iglesia De Dios on Summer Street while my father prayed.

I grew up a musician in the church. Back then, it was common for a few of us kids to sit in the front row and either idolize the drum player or play the congas or cowbell. I started with the cowbell and eventually, with the help of my grandmother, who would let me bang the pots and pans in the kitchen, worked my way up to playing drums. I also remember giving my first sermon in the church when I was about ten. In those days I and many of my friends mimicked some of the leaders in our church, including my father, who had by then cemented himself as an up-and-coming preacher and teacher. I remember being nervous at the beginning of my sermon but afterward frustrated with myself for not preparing as well as I should have.

Unlike Webber, I grew up in a classical Pentecostal fundamentalist tradition. In truth, I remember always being annoyed with the legalistic conservatism (holiness), which did not allow me to go to the movies, get a certain type of haircut, or even grow facial hair. As a child growing up in a populated industrial city, I never understood why my sisters had to wear skirts to places such as the beach and why our first movie theater experience (*Ninja Turtles*) was met with disdain. I cannot say that I remember much of the biblical teaching in those days. As a teenager, I suffered from a repressed individuation as a result of my legalistic upbringing, which caused me to act out inordinately.

I may have grown up with legalistic and sometimes repressive doctrinal teaching regarding dress and public appearance, but there was a unique supernatural spirituality embodied by the church on Summer Street. This type of spirituality usually came through worship and preaching and embodied the miraculous acts evidenced in the book of Acts. No one can ever convince me that I did not see people healed after our pastor, one Sunday morning, stood in front of one of the side windows of the church and asked all who were sick to come in contact with his shadow. I can also still remember sitting in the front row and witnessing a young woman come up for prayer, and afterward she began to sweat oil from her pores for days. Speaking of oil, I was there when the walls of the sanctuary began to drip oil, and miracles, signs, and wonders took place within the life of the congregation. All of these things occurred within the context of a church in the '80s and early '90s that had also adopted a monastic dedication for prayer and fasting. Years later, it was this exposure to the supernatural that held me during my darkest moments, bringing me back to prayer and once again stirring up in me both the fruits and the supernatural gifts of the Spirit.

Sometime after this, in the mid-nineties, my father was called to pastor a small church in Rochester, New York, and even though I lived with my grandparents, I pleaded to come along with him. And so, at eleven or twelve years old, I moved away from my three sisters, my grandparents, and the only city that I had ever known, my beautiful Paterson. Even today, going back makes me nostalgic.

Rochester was a place of cold and snow, which I had not been accustomed to. This reality was also met with a strict monastic-like prayer regiment enforced by my father. In the beginning of his pastorate, we lived in the apartment upstairs from the tiny storefront church on the corner of Bay Street. Every morning, he would wake me up at about 6 a.m., demanding that I join him in prayer, and yes, this included schooldays. I did not know it back then, but through my father's example, I later on learned how to develop a prayer life of my own.

My father's pastorate in Rochester ended after about four or five years. A new building, with a growing congregation, still stands after many years as a testament of his resolve and vision. Afterwards, he was called to Stamford, Connecticut, where he served over twenty years in a congregation of Central and South American believers.

A Searching but Painful Faith

Aside from the legalism, I never really had any other issues with what I experienced in the church growing up; I only had an issue with what I believed. During my early teenage years of individuation, this conflict in part led me to leave my family. While still a minor I plunged into the world of drugs, crime, and homelessness, eventually having to move out of the state of Connecticut and back to Rochester. Those days, although filled with hunger, embarrassment, and struggle, were also filled with angelic interventions and the leading of the Spirit, things I experienced then but only understood later. Even though back then I was in the midst of illegalities and depraved behavior, I still sensed a desire for an identity rooted in spirituality, and so I looked to other religions for help. Eventually I found myself practicing an African Yoruba religion that stressed live animal and material sacrifices to several deities.

I can see now that my acting out as a teenager was a plea for help, mixed with anger toward parental figures and my anger toward God and his church. Bishop Johnny Ray Youngblood, in speaking of Cain and Abel, often tells me that Cain should not be tried for murder but for manslaughter because he really was angry with God and, in trying to hit him, missed and hit Abel instead. At the time, it was inconceivable that the same miracle-working God whom I had experienced as a child was the same God of legalism that my parents had been serving. After some time, however, close to my twenties, I could run, hide, and be angry no longer.

My father, in sharing his conversion story, tells of a night while working at the casino in Atlantic City when he felt the room he was in begin to shake, and a voice along with a brilliant and magnificent light drowned the room. Years later, as a man not yet in my twenties, I shared a similar experience. One day, as I prepared to go to work in the kitchen of a restaurant where I had been employed for a few months, I sensed a familiar warmth going through my body, accompanied by an overwhelming desire to cry. Almost instinctively, I attempted to entertain my mind with other thoughts in hopes of distracting myself from what was occurring. While at work, I asked if the radio could be played louder. Then it happened. Fred Hammond's "No Weapon Formed against Me" came on the secular radio station, and what I had begun to feel at home all of the sudden fell on me, accompanied by a voice that kept saying, "I love you." My coworkers, assuming I had had a mental breakdown, drove me home. The next morning anything that had to do with my life the day before that was of an illicit nature was thrown away, including my pagan religious artifacts.

I do not remember there being any vagueness in me regarding my plans for the rest of my life the day after my conversion experience. I do not recall wanting to immediately preach, teach, or lead, but I do remember sensing as though this was going to be my ultimate destination. Perhaps it had to do with the many words of knowledge received as a kid regarding my call into ministry. Whatever the case may have been, I do remember wanting to learn as much of the Bible as possible. Ironically, after my experience at the restaurant, I went back to the church my father pastored in upstate New York, and from there went on to a church in Buffalo. Those years were the golden spiritual years of my life. It was there, living in the cold basement of a church in Buffalo, I learned how to pray, fast, and read the Scriptures.

Last but not least, I learned about the indwelling presence and working of the Holy Spirit.

Some years later, I found myself married with a child, working a secular job, preaching as an itinerant, and enrolled in a Bible school all at the same time. In those days, the miracles I experienced in my own traveling ministry mirrored those I had seen in my earlier years at the Iglesia de Dios on Summer Street. I had then an unceasing thirst for theological formation. Eventually, at twenty-one, after what I would call a series of extenuating circumstances, I found myself pastoring my first church.

I have pastored on and off in upstate New York for almost all of my twenty-plus years in the pastorate. Many of my inconsistencies in the early stages of pastoral ministry had to do not only with immaturity as a person and a pastor but with a conflict in my belief system. I vividly remember constantly asking myself, What do I believe? After some time of not being able to answer the question on my own, I took on other people's belief systems in an attempt to fill the void, only to be frustrated and abandon those systems altogether. In those days I experienced a multitude of diverse expressions that ranged from fundamentalist evangelicalism to third-wave Pentecostalism in the apostolic and prophetic movement, and everything in between. Yet, with every new experience, even though I was pastoring, I felt further and further away from God and his church.

In 2004, four years after I had started my first church, I was ordained into full-time ministry. At the ordination service, which was for others as well as for me, the preacher for the night, Bishop David M. Copeland, made a startling statement that shook my very being. While preaching on the nature of Christ and the church he stated, "Many people know Jesus, but they don't know the church." Upon hearing his statement, I immediately sat forward in my seat and asked myself, *What does he mean, know Jesus but not the church? Isn't that the same thing? Doesn't knowing one imply that you automatically know the other?* Unfortunately, I was not able to seek clarification from the bishop that night, but his statement brought both a light and at the same time a darkness to my crisis of faith.

This was the crisis of faith I was experiencing in 2005 while pastoring a small but growing church in one of the most impoverished neighborhoods in upstate New York. I can remember standing behind a makeshift Communion table that served as an audio-video table except on the first Sunday of the month. The table was draped with a purple cloth, two glass candlestick holders were placed at opposite ends of the table, and a silver Communion tray with a cross on the cover was in the center of the table, between the two candles. The tray of course held the little Communion cups with grape juice on the bottom and the bread directly above. Also on the table were two pewter chalices I had purchased from the local Christian bookstore, along with a small finger bowl of water. I remember wearing a black and purple robe fashioned by one of the best seamstresses in upstate New York, along with an amethyst ring and pectoral cross I had purchased from an online vendor. The rest of the church's clergy were dressed in black cassocks with purple stoles fashioned by the same person. Already positioned behind the table, the praise and worship team began to transition the music to something more somber in preparation for Communion. Right in that transition, I had a moment of deep spiritual crisis.

As the lights begin to dim and the first stanza of the song for Communion was about to be sung, I found myself looking directly at the table, beginning to despise the mechanical and rote actions I was about take. In that moment a flood of questions and doubts overtook my mind. *What am I doing? How do I remember Jesus' sacrifice for me? I never saw it, and I wasn't there two-thousand-plus years ago! What do the actions I am about to take all mean? Furthermore, what is up with the stale little wafers and the grape juice cups that have been left in a closet somewhere and a month later dug up and placed in this tray? Is this what the cross means? Is this what all the songs about Jesus' blood mean? Is this how the church has always done it, or is there more than just this?*

Suddenly, as though I had been abruptly transported back to the present from some place deep in outer space, the praise and worship team's voices were present in my hearing again. I looked around at the people, who by this time had been looking on with concern, and I raised the bread and wine, paraphrased the words of institution, ate together with them, and sat down awaiting the announcements. Without knowing, I had totally zoned out. Afterward I was told that I had been behind the table looking directly at it for over ten minutes with a blank stare.

That day, after the service was over and after assuring my congregation that I was indeed all right, I went home and became mildly depressed. I wrestled the entire week with what I had experienced that Sunday. Finally, after a week of sensing that something had awoken in me but not knowing what, I began my search for answers.

THE CONVERGENCE WORSHIP MOVEMENT

In 2006, during a conversation with Rick Hatfield, was the first time I heard the word *convergence*. Rick, a priest in the Charismatic Episcopal Church, was my professor for a course I was taking at an online school and had this day called to check up on my progress in the class. After a few pleasantries, I respectfully asked him to pray for me and explained that for about a year, I had been experiencing a crisis of faith. After listening to me patiently, Rick exclaimed, "I think the Lord is calling you into convergence." Afterward, he asked for my address, stating that he wanted to send me two resources that were not on my syllabus for the course but that would aid me in journeying through what I was experiencing. The first book was Thomas Howard's *Evangelical Is Not Enough*, and the second was Robert E. Webber's *Evangelicals on the Canterbury Trail*.[5]

I began to read both books while on a flight to Central America. I started with *Evangelical Is Not Enough*, and by the time I had finished with chapter one I had dismissed Howard's whole premise as idolatrous blasphemy. I was so angered by his perspective that I reached for my bag in the overhead bin and swapped his book for Webber's. A few sentences into Webber's book, however, I understood that I had gone from the pot into the frying pan, and so I switched back. During a five- to seven-hour flight I managed to read Howard's entire book, adding comments in the margins as I went along. My heart banged inside my chest as I read Howard's description of liturgical and sacramental worship, and even his chapter on the Virgin Mary began

---

[5]Webber, *Evangelicals on the Canterbury Trail*; Howard, *Evangelical Is Not Enough*.

to make sense to me—in short, I was hooked! After landing at the airport in Central America and upon arriving at the hotel, I immediately called Rick from the hotel lobby and shared how excited I was about what I had just read. Rick congratulated me, told me to read Webber's book as well, and promised to discuss both readings with me as soon as I returned back home.

Two weeks later, after arriving back home, settling in, and returning to my normal ministerial routines, I called Rick, but he did not answer. A few weeks later I received a general email from Rick sent out to all of his students. In it, he told us that he was ill and needed some time to treat his condition but that he did not believe his illness was going to overtake him. Sometime after his initial email, we received another email, this time from his wife. She informed us that the Reverend Canon Rick Hatfield had transitioned to be with the Lord on January 6, 2007. I was devastated. I did not know Rick personally—in fact, I had not even met him in person—but he was the first to ever take my crisis of faith seriously and give it direction, and for that I will forever be grateful to him. Memory eternal!

Sometime after Rick's transitioning, I found myself online seeking direction and guidance, and I ran across a convergence church just an hour from me called St. Patrick's. The church was affiliated with the Charismatic Episcopal Church and was headed by Father Kevin Baker, a priest and an astute businessman who for many years was the chief financial officer at Monks' Bread, run by the Trappist monks of the Abbey of Genesee in western New York. After my initial contact with Father Kevin, we agreed to sit for some coffee to discuss my journey. That day Kevin brought with him the book *The Christian Priest Today* by Archbishop Michael Ramsey.[6] Till this day, I treasure the copy he gave me and thank him for the incredible words of guidance and encouragement he imparted to me. He is now a priest in the Union of Charismatic Orthodox Churches, planting a church in Australia.

After the meeting, Kevin and I had a few more online and phone discussions. He ultimately introduced me to the patriarch of the Charismatic Episcopal Church, Archbishop Craig Bates, whom I met for lunch after

---

[6]Michael Ramsey, *The Christian Priest Today* (Eugene, OR: Wipf and Stock Publishers, 2012).

attending Mass at the Cathedral Church of the Intercessor in Malvern, New York. There I had my first real experience with how charismatic, liturgical/sacramental, and evangelical worship could be amalgamated. Mass seemed to be right of out of the book of Revelation, with worship from people of every nationality, incense as prayers, and at the center of it all the Eucharist. There I first experienced the reality of "real presence" at the table of the Lord.

While others have come to the concept of real presence through faith and or propositional biblical truths, I came to real presence through experience. I can remember that day walking up to the altar and sensing a warmth that covered my entire body. As I received the bread and the wine from the celebrant, and I crossed myself and uttered under my breath "I believe," I began to feel as though something had covered me. It was a reassuring feeling, similar to being given a coat in the midst of a brutal winter. Walking away from the altar back to my seat, I knew that I had experienced something, or better yet, someone. That experience still remains for me one of the closest I have had to heavenly worship.

After my meeting with Bishop Bates, there were some discussions about attending some Charismatic Episcopal Church leadership meetings as a guest, but unfortunately things did not really pan out. Our relationship, however, has continued to blossom over the years. Bishop Bates continues to be a wonderful friend and counselor.

The American Saint Patrick

Another year had almost passed after coming into contact with Father Baker and the Charismatic Episcopal Church, and aside from the resources I had studied, I had no real guidance or context from which to practice my newfound liturgical and sacramental faith. Then I received a call from Archbishop Paul Wayne Boosahda, also known as the American Saint Patrick. Boosahda is a tall, slender but strong man with Cherokee roots. Both his hair and beard are completely white (like depictions of Saint Patrick), he loves nature, and he is very fond of the mystical and relational nature of Celtic spirituality. I had not remembered, but during my time of searching for guidance and contacts, along with reaching out to Father

Kevin, I had also reached out to Bishop Boosahda by way of his website. One afternoon, after I was feeling like giving up my search, he called. By this time I was suspect of everyone. It was not that people had tried to do me harm in any way but rather that I did not want people thinking that I was reaching out to try to become a bishop. As far as I can remember, mine was a genuine yearning for knowledge and experience. Besides, at this time I was already a bishop within a major classical Pentecostal organization.

I took the phone call outside to the small front lawn of my house. His voice was fatherly but stern. He spoke with conviction but also caution. After conversing for about an hour, before closing our call, we agreed to have several more conversations regarding my journey, passion for ministry, family life, and education. A few months later, after assuring himself that our relationship had been God's will, Bishop Boosahda asked me if I had been feeling led to study for holy orders, to which I responded in the affirmative. For the next year and half, the American Saint Patrick took me through an intensive formational process, which included the reading of more than sixty theological, historical, and liturgical resources. The completion of each book had to be accompanied by a written essay, which we would discuss the week after. This classical formational process included works from the various Christian traditions (Anglican, Roman Catholic, Eastern Orthodox, Methodist, and so on) and covered various eras of time—patristic (apostolic, Nicene, and post-Nicene), medieval, Reformation, and so on. Upon completion of the reading and writing, I was also asked to complete a one-hundred-page canonical examination.

In that year and a half of intensive formation, I learned more about the historical church, its theology, and its worship than at any other time before. At that time that I also found an affinity for a distinctive pentecostal perspective on sacramentality. Even though I could not fully develop all my thinking then, I knew there had to be a way that pentecostals could engage orthodoxy.

Shortly after the bulk of my ministerial and theological formation with Bishop Boosahda, I was ordained a deacon and then a priest in the Communion of Evangelical Episcopal Churches (an organization I am no longer with but remain grateful to). I remember laying prostrate on the floor covered totally by a white pall, which is a liturgical cloth usually used to signify the persons death, while ministers gathered around me, praying for the Holy Spirit to descend on me. My youngest son, Lucas, who was five or six at the time, lay beside me in the same posture. This was unlike any other ordination that I had seen or experienced, and although I had studied holy orders in and out, nothing could compare to the sense of the Holy Spirit coming upon me, configuring me, and preparing me for the work ahead.

THE HARD ROAD

Lest anyone think that event's bliss carried over into weeks and months of ecstasy, the very week I was ordained I began to feel the pressure from some family members, colleagues, and friends. However, I reveled in finally having a creedal identity and a historic worship that did not need to always be made up. In fact, I remember that during my first theological class for my master's degree, when asked to write my faith statement by the professor, I took pride in writing down the Nicene Creed (the professor did not take too kindly to this simple response). But I had felt almost all alone in ministry for so long, and now I finally felt as though I belonged to something after exploring every Christian movement under the sun. I finally belonged to the church catholic. I was sharing in the belief and worship of Ignatius, Irenaeus, Athanasius, and others. As for some family, friends, and parishioners openly and secretly disagreeing with me, I did not mind; I just reminded myself of the many martyrs who came before me.

Over the next few years, I began to build churches that were fully sacramental, pentecostal, and evangelical. We would have a procession and go into ecstatic worship interspersed with the daily readings; I would preach, teach, and whoop, then call people to the altar for prayer and then celebrate the Eucharist. I lost many church members in those days. It was not so much that they did not enjoy me teaching them the things I had learned. In fact, most were excited about the teaching—the rediscovery of African Christianity, the contextual liturgy, the biblical and historical evidence of the sign of the cross, the biblical evidence for the real presence at the Eucharist, the historic iconoclast fight and the biblical evidence for icons—it was all there.

I taught week in and week out for years, yet despite all the teaching, it was still too "Catholic" for some.

I cried a lot during those days. I became depressed almost every Sunday looking at people's faces, some without interest in the Eucharist. Some visitors would even get up and leave right after the sermon because they knew that the celebration of the Eucharist was after the preached word. I can remember noticing the difference in the faces of some of the people between their reaction to the word preached and the celebration of the Eucharist. One minute they were screaming and shouting, running and clapping, and the next it seemed as though they could not get out of the building fast enough. I remember privately crying, asking myself, Why would people just want a good word but not want to eat of the very word they just heard? Why were they so quick to "plead the blood of Jesus" when there was not a single Bible verse that commanded Christians to do so, but there was ample biblical evidence for drinking his blood, and yet they did not want to do that? Oh, and I must remember to bring up the good ol' fight against real wine, the argument from members being that Jesus did not use real wine at the Last Supper or the wedding at Cana; it was really grape juice.

Arguments such as these are the ones that, since the later part of 2006, have helped me to understand how ingrained and rooted a particular perspective can be within segments of Christianity. I often say that, today, that which we are commanded to do, we do not do, but that which we are not commanded to do, we do!

After so many years of reflection on how recovering orthodoxy provided me with a sense of belonging (saints, martyrs, and so on), along with a sense of proper and directed worship (liturgy, church calendar, sacraments, and so on), I can truly say that none of these areas have been recovered at the expense of my pentecostalism. I still speak in tongues, believe in miracles, believe in the baptism of the Holy Spirit. I still believe in the direct work and experience of the Holy Spirit, in fact now more so than ever! After about ten years of identifying myself as convergence, I decided to ask myself why I just could not return to the tradition of my youth, bringing along with me my spiritual experiences and wealth of historic ecclesial knowledge.

Not much has changed. Today, I pastor a wonderful pentecostal/charismatic nondenominational church that recovers the Great Tradition within the Afro-Latino context under the umbrella of the Union of Charismatic Orthodox Churches. The Union of Charismatic Orthodox Churches, although a recent development, was built after five years of prayer and reflection to gather together segments of pentecostals recovering the Great Tradition under an autocephalous structure with a shared liturgy. I have been honored to sit and converse with so many wonderful men and women from so many different Christian traditions, yet at the end of the day I have decided that no trail can help me be the best bridge that I can be other than the pentecostal trail.

Lest my story be considered an isolated incident, I have asked other Pentecostal believers, most of whom have walked with me on this journey, to share their own stories of recovery. My hope is that through their stories as well as mine, readers will be encouraged and strengthened on their journey.

TABITHA PEREZ

It happened in a smoky chapel on the grounds of a retreat center in the middle of nowhere. There were voices reciting liturgy and song projecting out against the walls, echoing into my ears. There were no microphones in sight—just voices, one single piano, sunlight piercing the chapel windows, creating patterns in the smoke, fire, wine, bread, water, a table, people. It was simultaneously familiar and foreign. This was the moment I began to see my nondenominational/evangelical upbringing as transportation into this Pentecostal orthodox movement, in which I could sense the moving of the Spirit and eat the body of Christ in the same service. I had to experience what I could not understand before I could believe it.

I was raised on the south side of Chicago. As I aspired to be a good Christian girl who happened to be raised in the inner city, many things were forbidden. I mostly understood the need for boundaries, and home felt like a safe haven from the craziness of the world around me. I am eternally grateful for my upbringing, but sometimes those same safe walls felt like a cage. Three houses down was a set of train tracks that I was so curious about. I wondered endlessly about where they went, what the trains carried, why they were so loud, what was on the other side of the tracks. I longed to explore the neighborhood on my bike like I had seen the kids in the suburbs do, but it was not safe. So I went only to the porch, in the front yard, and in the backyard. I was safe, sheltered, confined.

My house was a religious one. We went to the church multiple times a week, and that pattern ramped up when there was a camp meeting or a revival happening. Our church was nondenominational, with evangelical influence, and even on occasion pentecostal (without any formal relationship with the denomination). Like youth in many churches in Chicago and across the country, I experienced it to be a warm and loving cocoon in which I was enveloped. The hands of the elders, the words of my mentors, the proclamation of my pastors, the admonition of prophets, and the lessons of Sunday school sheltered me in the same way that my home did. I am eternally grateful for the church of my youth, but I often felt caged. My community was insular, suspicious of denominationalism, and often judgmental of other expressions of worship (mainly ritualism and religious practices). Consequently, I only attended my home church, the affiliated churches, and the places where my pastor was on the program. Front yard, backyard, porch.

When I was twenty-five I decided to leave the church of my youth and join another congregation. This new pastor, called a bishop (a change of terminology for me), talked about Communion differently and wore what I now know as liturgical wear. In so many ways I was pressing at the boundaries of my youthful prohibitions. There was a set of "train tracks" that I was forbidden to cross or even to approach, and in my very early adulthood, I had taken a step outside the realm of the allowable. It was the most frightening thing I had ever done. My entire family still attended the previous church, and because of the aforementioned boundaries, it was the only church I had ever known in life. The new church had a different embodiment of worship, and I just could not resist. It was thoroughly Pentecostal (with affiliation this time), familiar and yet so different.

After a few years, this church began the journey backward into ancient Christianity. It was jarring. The bishop began to teach on the sacraments, the early church, and the church fathers. All of these topics had been in my periphery, but I had never invested diligent focus on them. As the bishop went through the classes, he took us through the topics he was learning. Afterwards, I also entered the Institute for Paleo-Orthodox Christian Studies (the program he had recently graduated). If the entirety of my life prior was characterized by prohibition and what I could not do, entering into this program was a radical step off the porch, past the front yard, and toward the train tracks of religious freedom for me. I had made the move with my body; my mind followed behind at a much slower pace.

I entered in through one of the intensives in which the student body met in Painted Post, New York, at a retreat center for a week to learn about ancient Christianity. To be clear, I was hesitant about the program to start. My tolerance for other forms of religious expression was low. There were certain roadblocks that I could not get past to see the truth in the message. Catholicism was my only framework for any ancient Christianity, and it was strictly forbidden and deemed witchcraft via messaging from my youth. I came to the intensive armed with an arsenal of subconscious platitudes that kept my mind sheltered even if my body had begun the journey toward the transportive nature of orthodox worship.

I am unsure of which Mass it happened at, what the homily was about, what songs were sung, or even whether it was at the first intensive or the second I attended. Details escape me, but I remember vividly that the chapel was smoky from the incense burning on the hot coal that the thurifer swung during the procession. I remember the sun pouring into the chapel windows, creating light patterns in the smoke, as I described at the beginning. I remember the echoes of voices hitting the walls and then back to my ears. I remember replaying the lessons in my mind that I had been learning over the week and seeing what the instructor had been saying. I remember the deacon proclaiming the gospel of our Lord. I remember partaking of the bread and wine and feeling the presence of God. It was familiar but so different. God had met me at this ancient ritual of communal worship around the table. The service then went into more familiar forms of spirituality such as prophecy and the laying on of hands.

At this service I began to understand my past differently. Learning about ancient Christianity makes it easy to devalue everything that is outside the scope of its prescriptive pattern. It is an alluring yet destructive inclination. It was precisely my evangelical upbringing that allowed me to recognize the moving of the Spirit in that fateful service in the chapel in New York. It was seeing the Pentecostal shouting and dancing that allowed me to understand the nature of embodiment in worship and thus made it easier for me to understand the need to bow and genuflect at the table. It was the altar call of my evangelical youth that allowed me to see that my participation in the service is my alignment with the heavenly intention—that I enter in with my mind, spirit, but also my body. I do not believe that evangelical/pentecostal worship is disembodied and ultimately doomed for spooky spirituality; rather, I believe that because of its divorce from ancient worship, the form of spirit-body connection changed. It is because of how I was raised that I can enter into a more orthodox way of worship and feel no separation between the natural and divine.

I have not said what was on the other side of the train tracks that were a few houses down from my childhood home. There was a bus garage there. Chicago has a bustling public transit system. The garages are where the buses go to change routes, park for the night, and get new routes. They are the brains of the entire transit system. Without drawing too fine a line under the metaphor, let us imagine the house, backyard, porch, and front yard are my spiritual upbringing, the tracks were the church I joined at twenty-five, and the bus garage ancient Christianity. Every part of the journey was valuable. In my youth I gained an understanding of the things of God, but just on the porch, and as I took the steps toward the other side of the tracks, I picked up things I needed to journey well into ancient Christianity. Now the church that I attend is a fully Pentecostal, fully ancient-faith congregation, and it is where I can go to rest, change, and do the work of him who sent me with my mind, spirit, and body. I am eternally grateful for those who led me on this journey: the pastor of my youth; the late Apostle Clifford E. Turner; Bishop David Maldonado; and my leader, teacher, and head of my diocese, Bishop Emilio Alvarez.

JAVIER VALDEZ

I was born in Guatemala City, Guatemala, on February 10, 1982, and immigrated to the United States at the age of two. My grandparents were of the faith and were active members of an Assemblies of God church, and as a result my family also grew to be followers of Christ. I was raised in a traditional Pentecostal/charismatic-centered environment where people speaking in tongues and shaking uncontrollably was the norm. In fact, if I were asked how Sunday service was, my reply would have been "unexciting" if these manifestations were not present. There was always an anticipation of these appearances in people, and if they were not visible, a majority of the congregants would feel as if the Sunday service were uninteresting or boring. We would only partake of the Lord's Supper occasionally, on Easter and Thanksgiving, and although my young years in this movement showed me what it was to seek God, how to pray passionately, and what it was to love my neighbor and help the needy, I was also subconsciously taught that this movement housed God himself, and anything outside it was not worth studying or investigating. In my young and ill-informed Christian walk I held on to this incorrect approach to Christianity and accordingly remained ignorant of other theological persuasions.

I did not begin to really understand the gospel until the age of sixteen in that church. As I began to develop my relationship with Christ, I had questions and curiosities about doctrine and church history that I brought up to my leaders, but because my inquiries were outside what our church believed or practiced, I was ultimately dismissed. My understanding of Christianity was ultimately wedged in the sixteenth century and attached to the view of *sola Scriptura* whereby any practice that I did not find in Scripture was abandoned or discarded. As a result, I became very suspicious of anything that was not followed by jumping, speaking in tongues, or trembling. Consequently, anything that remotely resembled Roman Catholicism was avoided entirely. It was frowned upon to associate with other believers who were not of our denomination or organization, and this left little to no room to experience spirituality in other traditions. For many years I served in that church as youth pastor. I will never say that my years in my traditional Pentecostal/charismatic church were lost years, but I do feel that I was robbed and restricted from the wealth of spiritual growth that came with spending time with other believers who practiced Christianity in different ways than I did.

While I continued to develop the call that God had over my life, I became an associate pastor of a nondenominational church. Although there was still speaking in tongues and uncontrollable shaking, I was able to advance in my journey with Christ. I developed new-members classes and led them quarterly. I was able to participate in worship services by preaching twice a month, and I oversaw the financial budget of the church. I was encouraged to share with other Christians, and I was able to meet people who opened up a plethora of opportunities for me to discover the spirituality that I practice now. My time at this church was quickly lived, and I left after three short years of serving there. It was there that I learned how not to lead a church.

As I grew in my studies and began to build strong connections with people from other Christian traditions, my journey with Christ truthfully began to flourish. I met Emilio Alvarez, who appropriately became my father in the faith and mentor. I enrolled in his Institute for Paleo-Orthodox Christian Studies, and in these settings my spirituality was truly alive and ongoing. Through these relationships and my studies I was able to recover in my spiritual walk the ancient faith and sacramental theology. I was drawn to the richness of the liturgy and the understanding that it was not some sort of outdated obstacle that removed my spontaneous prayer life. Liturgy was not just some vain repetition, as I was originally taught; it told a story, a really good story, a story about salvation and God's constant pursuit of me. What was even more amazing about this story, though, was that I was part of it, I was an active character in this divine re-creation, and this "vain repetition" was retelling over and over a story that was holisti-cally centered in God. Liturgy interrupts my reality daily and refocuses it on God. It does not negate our current culture; it just creates another one, a richer one where we can relish the goodness of God. I was on a quest for authentic spirituality that was beyond the physical feelings that I was used to. It was as if I had uncovered something that was in plain sight for so many and I was blind to it.

Around the same time, I discovered the church calendar and was engulfed in the wealth of spirituality found within it. My life revolves around calendars: work calendars, family calendars, and sports calendars, and because I am in this world I have to consider these. However, I discovered that although I am in this world, I am not of this world, and accordingly I should not forsake my true calendar, the church calendar. It is the church calendar that, instead of reminding me about meetings or weather forecasts, aims at changing the way I experience time and perceive reality. My days are now reshaped and concerned with the life of Jesus.

As I studied the life of the church fathers and their teachings, the way I conducted ministry was transformed through the lens of a consensual Christian viewpoint. I was no longer simply content with what the Scriptures said; I wanted to know what those who were in close proximity to Jesus and his apostles had to say about Scripture. I wanted to read their writings and learn about their lives.

While it is my understanding that not everything in the Scriptures is of equal weight, there are fundamental principles found therein that to me are not debatable. These principles are what have become essential to my faith:

- belief in God the Father, Jesus Christ, his Son, and the Holy Spirit
- the life, death, and resurrection of Jesus Christ
- the communion of the church and her saints
- the advent of Jesus Christ and salvation of his church

Although after all these years my principles have not changed, my theological understanding of these essential tenets over the past five years has changed considerably, albeit through continual scriptural study, reflection, and prayer.

JARED RUDDY

Sacramental Pentecostal. At one time I did not believe these two words could be spoken together, let alone become a defining phrase in my Christian life. Being a fourth-generation Pentecostal minister, my story stretches back to the dirt floors of a Maine revival where my great grandparents experienced the baptism of the Spirit at an Aimee Semple McPherson tent meeting. Because of this newfound experience, they were given the "left foot of fellowship" and were promptly booted out of their church. So, along with other early pioneers of Pentecostalism, they sacrificed comfort and certainty in order to be on the forefront of what God was doing at the turn of the century in North America.

Fast-forward four generations and a century later. As a Pentecostal kid growing up in the late '90s, I never had to worry about being kicked out of a denomination. By this time, Pentecostalism had spread to become the fastest-growing Christian movement in the world, accompanied by conferences, Bible colleges, seminaries, music festivals—you get the picture.

So, instead of having to face the fear of being kicked out of something, I was raised, dare I say entrenched, in the fact that I was proud to be a Pentecostal. I was part of a global movement of people who loved Jesus passionately and followed the Holy Spirit's leading faithfully.

As I reflect on those earlier years, I now realize there was an innate skepticism that accompanied my upbringing. No, not a questioning about tongues, or healings, or miracles, but rather a skeptical eye toward anyone who claimed to believe in Christ but did not champion the supernatural gifts of the Spirit. Take Catholics, for instance. Subtly, I embraced the belief that anyone who did not see the full expression of charismata in their church was stuck in empty, religious ritual or, worse yet, a form of godliness that denied the power thereof. Of course, this position was solidified by some hurtful interactions with a few Catholics who made fun of me for being a Pentecostal preacher's kid. As a result, my young heart found it convenient to believe that we Pentecostals had the real thing while other Christian traditions were just that—tradition.

This belief held true for me until after graduating from ministry school and planting a church at the age of twenty-one. Yes, twenty-one! After all, as a Pentecostal, I was raised to believe God would pour out his Spirit on the *young* and the old. Yet, as I led our newly founded church, my heart began to hunger, and I found myself especially drawn toward the Lord's Table. Like many Pentecostals, the church in which I grew up typically shared Communion on the first Sunday of the month. I had no real paradigm for the Supper, other than it was a place where I was to *remember* what Jesus did on the cross. But now, the drawing I sensed from the Holy Spirit was not merely about *remembering* what God had done in the past. Along with this came a profound awareness that Jesus desired to commune with me in the present through this covenant meal. Although I had no developed theology for this, I could sense the Holy Spirit's leading, wooing me to the Lord's Table in the same way as I felt him draw me to the altar for prayer when I was a child.

Years later, as I now lead a historic Pentecostal church, we joyfully celebrate the Lord's Supper in each of our weekly services. Far from what I once believed to be empty tradition, many in our church find the Table to be the place where they sense God's presence. In hindsight, I should not be surprised that the Holy Spirit has led me to the Lord's Table. The Spirit, after all, was given to us to lead us to Jesus. And Jesus gave us the Eucharist in order to meet with us through broken bread and poured-out wine. While I am only a few years into my sacramental journey, my Pentecostalism is more active and alive than ever. The one has not excluded the other, but both have been enhanced. Now, instead of viewing sacramental ministry as dry, religious tradition, I see time-tested wells that God has made available so every thirsty soul may draw from them and drink. While my inner Pentecostal still believes you can *find* God anywhere, I have made the glad discovery that he promises to *meet* us at his Table. *Sacramental Pentecostal*—two words I never thought would go together have become for me an inseparable way of life.

4

TOWARD AN AFRO-LATINO
PENTECOSTAL ORTHODOXY

HANGING ON THE WALL in my church office is an unconventional picture of the Last Supper by artist Sieger Koeder. What makes it unconventional are the people sitting around the two nail-pierced hands, seemingly gazing into the face of an unseen Jesus. They look nothing like the traditional Da Vinci painting we are used to in the West. In contrast to Da Vinci's painting of the Last Supper, where there are mostly white men who seem to be part of the upper echelon of their time, Koeder's painting is inclusive of people of color, women, and even the wounded and bruised.[1] To the left, there are drawings of people on the wall, which seem to have been done in chalk, and far off at the end of the table across from Jesus' hands one can see a stone-faced, shadowy gray figure who almost seems as though he is surrounded by darkness. One can only imagine that this figure represents Judas Iscariot, who went on to betray Jesus.

I have often found myself losing myself for minutes on end imagining the premise for this work of art. I have gazed at it intently many times, wondering about the artist's motivation, vision, and worldview. Who are these men and women? How did they get there? How did men and women of color get to come to one on the most iconic tables in human history?

---

[1]See www.shutterstock.com/tr/image-photo/san-pastore-italy-circa-february-2017-616095647, detail of the Last Supper (Abendmahl) by Sieger Koeder in refectory of Villa San Pastore in Italy.

The question I have posed for the painting is the same question I have asked myself regarding segments of an Afro-Latino pentecostalism recovering the Great Tradition. How did we get here? How did we get to come to the Table, both figuratively and literally? Even more importantly, what if people of color have always been there and have been relegated to the margins? What if Koeder's depiction is accurate and Da Vinci's is not?

This chapter looks to explore the present experience of Afro-Latino pentecostals recovering the Great Tradition within a North American context. It deals primarily with Black and brown pentecostal clergy and ecclesial institutions in the story of recovery. How and why are elements of orthodoxy becoming attractive to Afro-Latino pentecostals, and what impact have the forms of white normativity had on Afro-Latinos recovering these elements of orthodoxy? What role can an early African Christianity play in combating a dominant European, white-normative perspective toward such a recovery?

TERMINOLOGY

Before engaging further, it is best to qualify what I mean when utilizing the term *Afro-Latino* or *Afro-Latinix*.[2] According to Leslie K. Best, *Afro-Latino* is used to primarily identify "a person who is Latino and of African heritage."[3] For Miriam Jiménez Román and Juan Flores, the term was "born and reared" within a "transnational crucible of struggle and self-affirmation," for "people of African descent in Latin America and the Caribbean."[4] Alejandro de la Fuente and George Reid Andrews define the field of Afro-Latin American studies "first as the study of people of African ancestry in Latin America, and second, as the study of the larger societies in which those people live."[5] Within the context of the United States the field of

---

[2]The term *Afro-Latinix*, in my opinion, is the best term that can adequately represent men and women from Latin America or the Caribbean who are also of African descent. Widely used in scholarly circles, the term is presently in the Merriam-Webster Dictionary, and is used to identify people of Latin America, the Carribean, or of African descent. The Merrriam-Webster Dictionary does not define Afro-Latinx as a social collective.

[3]Leslie K. Best, *The Afro-Latino: A Historical Journey* (Matteson, IL: Besslie Books, 2010), vii.

[4]Miriam Jiménez Román and Juan Flores, *The Afro Latin@ Reader: History and Culture in the United States* (Durham, NC: Duke University Press, 2010), 2.

[5]Alejandro de La Fuente and George Reid Andrews, *The Making of a Field: Afro-Latin American Studies; An Introduction* (New York: Cambridge University Press, 2018), 1.

Afro-Latino studies, according to Jimenez and Flores, has to do with the "distinctive and unique phenomenological experience lived at a personal level by people who are both Black and Latin@ in all aspects of their social life."[6] Jimenez and Flores go on to suggest that the field embodies the

> cross-cultural relation between the Afro and the Latin@ which means most saliently the relation between Latin@s and African Americans. Thus while the concept refers first of all to the group experience of Black Latin@s themselves, the broader interaction between the two "largest minorities," including non-Afro Latin@s and non-Latin@ Blacks bears directly on that population that is both and conditions its social experience at every stage.[7]

In utilizing the term *Afro-Latino*, this book means to do so primarily in a secondary sense, as a collective, sociologically referring to an African American or Latino American group or community whose identity and spirituality is rooted in the African diaspora. One reason to use *Afro-Latino* as a social collective is that colonialism and slavery have had a similar negative effect on the Afro-Latino pentecostal perspective concerning what is deemed as "Catholic" and ultimately "white." Another reason is the racial disparities for African Americans as well as Latinos in the United States, which are also often similar. This has been particularly true in the southern states. Ramona Houston states, "Throughout its history, [the history of the southern states in America], African Americans and Latinos have been subjected to similar forms of racialization, segregation and discrimination which in turn, have produced some of the same social, political and economic issues within each of these communities."[8] Houston calls for an Afro-Latino coalition based on intergroup commonalities that supports collaboration between the two groups. Given the similarities of racial and social designation, we can speak of an Afro-Latino community as a group of individuals who are either African American or Latino American with an African heritage.[9]

---

6. Jiménez Román and Flores, *Afro Latin@ Reader*, 14.
7. Jiménez Román and Flores, *Afro Latin@ Reader*, 12.
8. Ramona Houston, "The Value of African American and Latino Coalitions to the American South," *Journal of Global Initiatives: Policy, Pedagogy, Perspective* 2, no. 1 (2010): 65.
9. Anyone seeking more information on the Africanness of Latin@s would do well in considering Jiménez Román and Flores, *Afro-Latin@ Reader*, as well as Herbet Klein and Ben Vinson, *African Slavery in Latin American and the Caribbean* (New York: Oxford University Press, 2007).

Although this chapter does not deal explicitly with a colonized Native American Indian reception of Christianity and its subsequent contribution to the religious life and spirituality of Afro-Latino/as in particular, this does not mean that such a reality never existed. In fact, a reading of Mark Christensen's *Translated Christianities* shows how trained Native American Indians developed a contextual Nahuatl Bible some time before 1560 even under great duress.[10] Amalgamated Christian tales and narratives such as Paul's conversion story are retold in a style that contrasts with what European Jesuits originally taught the Native converts, proving that in the Americas there has always existed the impulse to interpret the gospel in a way that is understandable to Native American Indian peoples, most of whom went on to become Afro-Latinos. Christensen's work is relevant to the conversation regarding the Africanness of Christian Afro-Latino pentecostals, especially during these times where many Latino/a Christians, especially evangelicals and pentecostals, seem to have become co-opted by a nationalist, amnesia-stricken historical narrative.

With the terminology in place, we can now turn to how and why the recovery of elements of the classical consensual tradition has become attractive to Afro-Latino pentecostals. It must be noted that in utilizing the term *elements* in regard to Afro-Latino pentecostals recovering the Great Tradition, I am simply referring to most of the cosmetic trappings (dress, rankings, and so on) of the Great Tradition, rather than its historic spirituality. These comments are in no way made to disparage Afro-Latino pentecostals but to show that for the most part there seems to be a progressive adoption of these base elements in combination with pentecostal spirituality. In fact, as I will examine, there seems to have always existed within early pentecostalism an impulse toward such a recovery.

AZUSA STREET MISSION

The Azusa Street revival started with African Americans, then moved into being biracial (Black and white), but ultimately ended up becoming a multiracial and multiethnic international movement with the help of Latinos

---

[10]Mark Z. Christensen, *Translated Christianities: Nahuatl and Maya Religious Texts* (Latin American Originals) (University Park, PA: The Pennsylvania State University Press, 2014).

and other immigrants. In fact, as Gastón Espinosa shows, both the first manifestation of the Spirit at Azusa and the first healing to occur at Azusa happened to a Latino of Mexican origin.[11] Therefore, Azusa can be considered, among many other things, an Afro-Latino Pentecostal movement. This distinction does not mean to discount the vital role and presence of Anglo brothers and sisters within the revival but rather simply looks toward the focus of this work.

Ecumenical connections seem to have been the vehicle from which early African American Pentecostals drew much of their organizational structure. Espinosa shows in his book *William J. Seymour and the Origins of Global Pentecostalism* how even Seymour himself, in constructing *The Doctrine and Discipline of the Azusa Street Mission*, drew from the African Methodist Episcopal Church's Book of Discipline, the 1801 Anglican Church's Thirty-Nine Articles of Religion, and other "apostolic letters and doctrinal statements." These early Methodist and Anglican influences seem to have also caused Seymour to change his views on various practical matters as well, including going from a congregational to an episcopal-style polity. In fact, one of the more interesting disciplines to note in Azusa Street's *Doctrine and Discipline* is Seymour's use of a seemingly Anglican rite for the consecration and ordination of elders, bishops, and deacons. The ordinations include a collect, Scripture readings, a public examination, and an epiclesis (invocation of the Holy Spirit), and end with the Lord's Supper. Seymour makes no distinction between elder and bishop in regard to rank or Christian ministry, except in regard to the "Superintendency in the Church."[12] Seymour, an early African American Pentecostal father, not only adopted what seems to be an episcopal polity but also adopted its historic ordination liturgy.

Seymour identifies the Lord's Supper, baptism, and footwashing as sacraments, a term not usually utilized by early Pentecostal believers because of its theological connections to Catholicism. For Seymour, the sacraments are signs of grace and strengthen and confirm the believer's faith in God.[13] It

---

[11]Gastón Espinosa, *William Seymour and the Origins of Global Pentecostalism: A Biography and Documentary History* (Durham, NC: Duke University Press, 2014), 59.

[12]Espinosa, *William Seymour*, 216, 268-81.

[13]Espinosa, *William Seymour*, 235.

must be noted, however, that for Seymour as well as for generations of Pentecostals after, the usage of the term *sacrament* does not necessarily imply the adoption of a theory of physical sacramental causality (effective of sacramental grace) rooted in the teaching of "real presence." Instead, as I suggested in chapter two, an early adoption of the term *sacrament* within early North American Pentecostalism most likely denotes a sacramental occasionalism that remembers the grace of God at the actual celebration of the rite.

In regard to baptism as a sacrament, Seymour sees it not only as a distinguishing sign of profession but as a sign of "regeneration or the new birth." Seymour's usage of the phrase "sign of" contrasts the earliest thinking regarding baptism as rebirth, as understood by the early patristic fathers (Justin Martyr, Tertullian, and so on). Pentecostals believe being born again is a result of a confession of faith occurring within a conversion experience outside baptism.[14] Concerning the Lord's Supper, although Seymour shuns the teaching of transubstantiation as unprovable by Scripture, he does stress that the body and blood of Christ are eaten "after a heavenly and spiritual manner," which necessitates faith.[15]

THE CHURCH OF GOD IN CHRIST

While the institutional longevity of the Azusa Street Mission may have been short lived (1906–1930), other early African American Pentecostal churches have continued to combine pentecostal spirituality with elements of the Great Tradition. The Church of God in Christ is probably the best example. Incorporated in 1897, the Church of God in Christ continues to be the most influential African American Pentecostal denomination of our time. Similar to the Azusa Street Mission, there seems to have been a small group of Latino congregations in the Church of God in Christ from the 1920s to the 1960s located within the western United States. Currently, the Church of God in Christ has churches in Brazil, Cuba, and a number of other Latin American countries as well.[16]

---

[14]See Allen Anderson, *An Introduction to Pentecostalism: Global Charismatic Christianity* (New York: Cambridge University Press, 2004); Veli-Matti Kärkkäinen, *The Spirit in the World: Emerging Pentecostal Theologies in Global Context* (Grand Rapids, MI: Eerdmans, 2009), 39.

[15]Espinosa, *William Seymour*, 236.

[16]Personal conversation with David Daniels, September 10, 2020.

The Reconstruction-era African American Holiness movement, built by William Christian, Charles Prince Jones, and Charles Mason, embodied a spirituality that "was carefully restructuring the engagement between Christian faith and modern society, balancing theological and liturgical innovations against contemporary traditions and customs, and quietly adopting dimensions of contemporary Baptist and Methodist life." In the early years of the African American Holiness movement these adoptions from Baptist and Methodist culture were mainly organizational and might help to explain to some extent the Church of God in Christ's adoption of a more historic clerical structure.[17]

The Church of God in Christ seems to have adopted early on the same style of organizational presbyterian-episcopal polity that Seymour did, using the term *bishop* as an ecclesial rank among its clergy. This is possibly due to its early exposure and relationship with the Methodist tradition through men such as Elder Robert E. Hart, who was a member of the Colored Methodist Episcopal Church before coming to the Church of God in Christ. Hart went on to be one of Mason's greatest supporters as well as the denomination's attorney, representing Mason and the Church of God in Christ in their case against C. P. Jones.[18]

At the Church of God in Christ's first general assembly in 1907, Mason was designated the denomination's general overseer and chief apostle. Later on he was designated the senior bishop of the church, "with absolute authority in matters of doctrine and church organization."[19] That the rank of bishop existed early within the Church of God in Christ as a whole is backed up by Clarence Taylor. Taylor, in referencing Brooklyn's Christian Antioch Apostolic Church of God in Christ's sixteenth anniversary in 1947, mentions its establishmentarian Samuel Williams, who "was given the title of bishop by the religious organization."[20]

[17]John M. Giggie, *After Redemption: Jim Crow and the Transformation of African American Religion in the Delta, 1875–1915* (New York: Oxford University Press, 2008), 170, 172.

[18]Calvin S. McBride, *Walking into a New Spirituality: Chronicling the Life, Ministry, and Contribution of Elder Robert E. Hart, B.D., LL.B., D.D., to the CME Church and COGIC; With Some Additional COGIC History* (New York: iUniverse, 2007), xix, xxi.

[19]Eric C. Lincoln and Lawrence H. Mamiya, *The Black Church in the African American Experience* (Durham, NC: Duke University Press, 1990), 81.

[20]Clarence Taylor, *The Black Churches in Brooklyn* (New York: Columbia University Press, 1994), 37.

The model of authority for the Church of God in Christ's senior bishop changed after 1968, when the convention did away with the office.[21] In 1972, the church's constitution was revised, making the General Assembly (General Board, all jurisdictional bishops, pastors and elders, supervisors, district missionaries, and lay and foreign delegates) the legislative and doctrinal authority of the church. The constitutional revision represents a change in ecclesial authority from a patriarchal model of sorts to a more presbyterian-type model of government. The church today retains a Board of Bishops, which is inclusive of all of the bishops in the church, and a General Board of Bishops, which is composed of twelve bishops and, along with the general assembly, is responsible for electing the presiding bishop from the general board.[22] This structure resembles the unity of bishops in a more Eastern, Cyprian, collegial manner. Bishops in the Church of God in Christ are for the most part given geographical jurisdictions over which they preside, and churches within those jurisdictions enjoy a healthy independence from their juridical leadership.

Although founded by a former Baptist minister, with some modifications to Methodist and Baptist organizational structure, some within today's Church of God in Christ can be seen using high-church liturgies along with Anglican vestments. This change, according to some in the COGIC, is said to have come sometime within the late 1970s into the 1980s, while J. O. Patterson, the first bishop to be elected by the General Assembly in 1968, was leading the church. Interestingly, J. Delano Ellis, founder of the Joint College of African American Pentecostal Bishops, is to some extent credited with being responsible for introducing Anglican vestments and high-church liturgy into contemporary Church of God in Christ culture.

Various pieces of information reveal an ongoing developmental understanding of the sacraments in the Church of God in Christ. For example, the articles of religion written in the 1930s, along with the 1940 manual of the Church of God in Christ, identify the Lord's Supper as a sacramental rite, speak of believers as "orthodox Christians," and make reference to the

---

[21]Wardell J. Payne, ed., *Directory of African American Religious Bodies: A Compendium by the Howard University School of Divinity*, 2nd ed. (Washington, DC: Howard University Press, 1995), 163.
[22]Lincoln and Mamiya, *Black Church*, 85.

"apostolic age." The 1973 manual speaks of the "ordinances" as signs of grace, addresses liturgical dress, makes reference to bishops during the apostolic and subapostolic age (including Clement and Ignatius), and includes both the Apostles' and Nicene Creeds.[23]

On its official website the Church of God in Christ uses the term *ordinances* to refer to the Lord's Supper, baptism, and footwashing.[24] However, a 2015 training manual for the National Adjutancy uses the term "Sacrament of Holy Communion" when referring to the Lord's Supper.[25] Once again, for the Church of God in Christ the term *sacraments* seems to be utilized with a theory of sacramental occasionalism in mind. Yet, elements of the Great Tradition have been included within the organization's ordering and ministerial documentation. Aside from all of the incredible work the Church of God in Christ does globally, one wonders what a Pentecostal organizational as large the Church of God in Christ could accomplish ecumenically and beyond if it was to recover more robust elements of the Great Tradition aligned with its Pentecostal spirituality (eucharistic epiclesis, African patristics, and so on).

THE AFRICAN ORTHODOX CHURCH

Although this chapter mainly deals with Afro-Latino pentecostals who are recovering elements of the Great Tradition, it would be unwise to ignore the fact that there is indeed precedence for an African American recovery of the Great Tradition in general. The African Orthodox Church serves as a prime example of a Black autonomous and independent church governed by persons of African descent who synthesize racial consciousness, maintain orthodox theology and apostolic order, and practice a catholic sacramental and liturgical worship that generally follows a Western rite.[26] The African Orthodox Church was founded in New York by former Episcopalian George Alexander McGuire in 1921

---

[23]*Church of God in Christ 1973 Manual* (Memphis: Church of God in Christ Publishing, 1973).

[24]"What We Believe," Church of God in Christ, www.cogic.org/about-us/what-we-believe/.

[25]Church of God in Christ, "National Adjutancy: The Service Ministry of the Church of God in Christ," 2015, www.cogic.org/adjutancy/files/2015/07/SNAC-2015-Training-Manual.pdf.

[26]William Platt, "The African Orthodox Church: An Analysis of Its First Decade," *Church History* 58, no. 4 (December 1989): 483.

and eventually spread as far as South, East, and West Africa by way of African American journal publications that reported on its mission and vision.[27] McGuire, according to William Platt, was "disappointed with the slow progress of the Negro in the Episcopal Church and the apparent indifference of that church to his race's aspirations for positions of leadership."[28] In speaking of "ecclesiastical slavery," McGuire comments, "Our perpetual lot is to remain doorkeepers in the Holy Catholic Church with the added privilege of gathering the crumbs which fall from our masters' table."[29] McGuire's disillusion with ecclesial race relations in the Episcopal Church at the time eventually led him to become heavily involved with Marcus Garvey and the Universal Negro Improvement Association, eventually serving as the organization's chaplain.

The organization, per its organizing documents, understands its usage of the designation "Orthodox" as its faith being "Orthodox, in conformity with the Orthodox Churches of the East from which its Episcopate is derived [a reference to McGuire's Episcopal ordination by Renee Villate who was excommunicated by the Syrian Orthodox Church before he consecrated McGuire]."[30] The organization does not see itself as a break from any church, nor as an expression of a new doctrine, but rather maintains that it was "an expression of the spirit of racial leadership in ecclesiastical matters, in harmony with the racial consciousness of the Negro people following the recent World's War."[31]

Although presenting itself as an Orthodox Church, the African Orthodox Church incorporated a mix of both Western and Eastern theological themes and practices, such as the acceptance of the Apostles', Nicene, and Athanasian Creeds, the Eastern rejection of the *filioque*, and the affirmation of the real presence of Christ in the Eucharist but through the framework of the Western doctrine of transubstantiation. The African Orthodox Church's

---

[27]Ciprian Burlaciou, "Expansion Without Western Missionary Agency and Constructing Confessional Identities: The African Orthodox Church Between the United States, South Africa, and East Africa (1921–1940)," *Journal of World Christianity* 6, no. 1 (2016): 84–87.

[28]Platt, "African Orthodox Church," 475.

[29]George Alexander McGuire, *The Negro Churchman* 1, no. 2 (1923): 1. McGuire reflected on his fate in the Episcopal Church and wrote his reflection in the Negro Churchman Journal.

[30]Platt, "African Orthodox Church," 483.

[31]A. C. Terry-Thompson, *The History of the African Orthodox Church* (New York: Beacon, 1956), 53.

liturgy, *The Divine Liturgy and Other Rites and Ceremonies of the Church*, has been described as a mixture of Anglican and Roman Catholic rites with a sprinkle of Greek Orthodox themes.[32] Clergy use Western-style vestments during the liturgy, and the liturgy itself, according to Platt, is "based upon a conflation of the Roman Missal and the Book of Common Prayer," in many ways mirroring the Mass of St. Tikhon.[33] Further examination could perhaps determine that the African Orthodox Church's eucharistic liturgy could meet Orthodox Western Rite standards with a few modifications. The African Orthodox Church's liturgy can serve as a blueprint for other African American organizations recovering the Great Tradition, which would lead to interesting and fruitful ecumenical dialogue.

One could have many conversations concerning the African Orthodox Church's view of valid apostolic succession or the historic legitimacy of its amalgamated liturgy. But what makes the African Orthodox Church pertinent here is that it represents possibly one of the first examples of the catholicity of the Great Tradition being reflected on through the lens of an African American racial consciousness. Not only that, but the African Orthodox Church also represents one of the first attempts at developing a branch of the non-Protestant "Catholic Church" for "Catholic people of color utilizing the designation 'Orthodox.'" F. A. Garrett, an archdeacon in the African Orthodox Church, in speaking of the African Orthodox Church as a branch of the Catholic Church for people of African descent, uses the term *Orthodox* as a culturally inclusive term. He states:

> We have the Russian Orthodox Church, for example; and again the Greek Orthodox Church; and still again the Syrian Orthodox Church; but none of these Churches claims to be the whole Catholic Church, but simply a part. . . . The Greek Orthodox Church is the Church for Greek Catholics, the Russian Orthodox Church for Russian Catholics, the Syrian Orthodox Church for Syrian Catholics and the African Orthodox Church for Colored Catholics.[34]

---

[32] *The Divine Liturgy and Other Rites and Ceremonies of the Church: According to the Use of the African Orthodox Church* (New York: 1923).

[33] Platt, "African Orthodox Church," 486.

[34] F. A. Garret, "Is the Title African Orthodox Correct?," *The Negro Churchman* 7, no. 1 (1929): 4.

According to Platt, the African Orthodox Church, after having analyzed the racial disparities of the American Christian church at the time, understood that the only avenue of redress for Black Christians was the creation of an independent and autonomous ecclesial body administered by Blacks and responding to the needs and aspirations of its Black constituencies. Interestingly, McGuire, although rebuffed by some Orthodox leadership, did eventually enter into some dialogue with the Orthodox ecumenical patriarch at the time, who took interest in the African Orthodox Church.[35] In this way McGuire and the African Orthodox Church continue to stand even today as models for an African American recovery of the Great Tradition in tension with a devout racial consciousness.

THE JOINT COLLEGE OF AFRICAN AMERICAN PENTECOSTAL BISHOPS

The Joint College of African American Pentecostal Bishops represents a more recent and subtle interest in the recovery of the Great Tradition on the part of Afro-Latino pentecostals. In 1993, four bishops of the Pentecostal community had a conversation regarding the need for training Pentecostal clergy for the office of the bishop.[36] Their founding narrative, "the legitimacy of the African American Pentecostal Episcopacy," was and continues to be its primary impulse toward the recovery of base elements of the Great Tradition. Their concern for African American clerical preparedness, in particular for the episcopal office in the Pentecostal tradition, motivated them to form an organization that later came to be known as the Joint College of African American Pentecostal Bishops. The Joint College, as it is often called,

> seeks to accomplish the implementation of [its] core values through a comprehensive training program offered yearly in March. The college also offers an Adjutant school, a Helpmeet and Episcopal companions forum, Episcopal Installation Services to Reformations; a Scholarship Program, and an

---

[35]See Theodore Natsoulas, "Patriarch McGuire and the Spread of the African Orthodox Church to Africa," *Journal of Religion in Africa* 12, no. 2 (1981): 89.

[36]"Who We Are," The Joint College of African American Pentecostal Bishops, accessed December 12, 2017, www.collegeofbishops.org/who-we-are.

International College event that reconnects the American Episcopacy with the global church.[37]

The late Archbishop J. Delano Ellis II (memory eternal) was the primate of the Joint College and helped it grow into what many in the African American pentecostal community consider to be "the premier development center for the Episcopacy in the African American culture specifically and the global Lord's church generally."[38] Ellis is responsible for the philosophical and practical development of the modern-day adjutancy, a concept he brought from his military experience into Pentecostal denominations and ecclesial organizations such as the Church of God in Christ and the Joint College.

Every year the Joint College attracts over six hundred clergy members to its conference, which represents over one million Christian believers in denominations around the world. As a form of Afro-Latino Pentecostal orthodoxy, the Joint College is still very much in the early stages of development. Members have adopted Anglican vestments, use Anglo-Roman clerical designations in order to distinguish clerical ranks, and boast of having both Eastern and Western lines of apostolic succession. To date, however, the understanding and recovery of the more foundational elements of conciliar or consensual orthodoxy (historical theology, liturgical worship, and sacramentality) remains limited. Most of the working written or presented material at the college seems to be devoid of key historic elements vital to the episcopacy.

However, there are shifts that seem to be slowly taking place within the ranks of the Joint College. Recently, teaching on sacramental theology had become commonplace at the Joint College's yearly session for freshman bishops, although I am not sure if this is still the case presently. One bishop, whom I had the pleasure of training, states, "While our journey as clergymen toward orthodoxy began with a desire both to better organize ourselves within the episcopacy and to recover our own social identity, this Spirit-led journey also is leading us, albeit slowly, into matters of creedal

---

[37]"Who We Are."
[38]"Who We Are."

identity along with a recovery of sacramental and patristic appreciation."[39] As an institutional instrumentality in the hands of an ecumenism of the Spirit, the Joint College does display an interdenominational unity rarely seen in other reformational networks or organizations. The Joint College has welcomed Methodists, Baptists, Pentecostals, and nondenominational clergy since its inception.

The important factor to keep in mind regarding these three examples is that there exists within early Afro-Latino pentecostalism and beyond an impulse toward the recovery of structural and base liturgical elements of the Great Tradition. This recovery seems to be limited to organizational structures, ordinations, clerical ranks, ecclesiastical vestments, and (as in the case of the Joint College) African American Pentecostal legitimacy.

Given the resembling narratives above, there are two pertinent questions that must be asked of Afro-Latino Pentecostals recovering these base elements of the Great Tradition. First, do they see themselves as Pentecostal bishops or bishops who are Pentecostals? This question is vital to both the identification and spirituality of any pentecostal organization looking to recover elements of the Great Tradition. To identify as a pentecostal bishop, as many within the organizations above do, would suggest that a spiritual movement that began in 1906, to some extent as a recapitulation of Acts 2, is the leading factor in ecclesial identification. If this is the case, then how can Afro-Latino pentecostal bishops who come from these organizations claim apostolic succession, seeing as how pentecostalism represents a more recent North American renewal movement? To speak, however, of bishops who are pentecostal places the sacramental emphasis of the episcopacy, along with its liturgical and sacramental spirituality, at the forefront of ecclesial identification. To be a bishop first, rightly formed, is to express an ecclesial spirituality in conjunction with a form of ecclesial leadership. To say that one is pentecostal first expresses a denominational identity that has been devoid of the reality of a historical episcopate inclusive of a sacramental/liturgical spirituality. This issue is vital not only for Afro-Latino pentecostals claiming

---

[39]Bishop in the Joint College of African American Pentecostal Bishops, phone interview with author, December 1, 2017.

apostolic succession but also for future ecumenical dialogues with other Christian traditions.

CATHOLIC EQUALS WHITE

The second question that must be raised of Afro-Latino Pentecostals recovering these base elements of the Great Tradition is, Why are classical consensual exegesis, historic liturgy, and sacramental spirituality and theology considered to be Catholic and distinct from or avoided by pentecostalism as a whole, as well as white and contrary to what people of color practice? Antipas Harris, in *Is Christianity the White Man's Religion?*, looks to affirm biblical Christianity's cultural diversity. The very question posed to Harris by one of his students, "What do you say to your friends who are leaving the church and arguing that Christianity is the white man's religion?"[40] according to Harris, "challenges a history in which groups of professing Christians have used the Bible in ways that oppress others. . . . The question of Christianity being a white man's religion expresses concern about pervasive white male ideology in society's structures."[41] Harris goes on to argue not only for a sobering biblical interpretive process that displays the Bible as culturally inclusive but for a debunking of several ideological perspectives (inclusive of white supremacy) that continue to affect negatively the way African Americans are depicted religiously.

Harris's argument is expanded by Vince Bantu. Bantu, in identifying an orthodoxy present within an African framework, argues,

> Many people in the modern world understand the concept of "orthodoxy"—especially Christian orthodoxy rooted in Scripture—as a facet of white supremacy and Western hegemony. . . . The practice of contending for orthodox belief based on the authority of Scripture is a long-held tradition among African Christians and is by no means an innovation of Western Christians.[42]

---

[40]Antipas Harris, *Is Christianity the White Man's Religion? How the Bible Is Good News for People of Color* (Downers Grove, IL: InterVarsity Press, 2020), 3.

[41]Harris, *Is Christianity the White Man's Religion?*, 16.

[42]Vince L. Bantu, *A Multitude of All Peoples: Engaging Ancient Christianity's Global Identity* (Downers Grove, IL: InterVarsity Press, 2020), 82.

As an Afro-Latino recovering the Great Tradition, I have discovered that this recovery is very often perceived to be colonialist, Catholic, and ultimately white. This connection between an ingrained Catholo-phobia and the suspicion of whiteness is a result of the complicated relationship between religion, colonization, and slavery, which has caused two distinct ecclesial responses on the part of Afro-Latino pentecostals. First, there exists a rebellion against a perceived white religious normativity. White normativity, as defined by Kathy Winings, is the "cultural practices, attitudes, assumptions, and ideologies in the wider society and culture using the white culture as the standard, the norm."[43] This reality is still connected to the history of both the rise of the African American church and the American system of slavery. In his book *Becoming an Anti-Racist Church*, Joseph Barndt states that in America,

> White slave masters taught slaves a twisted and distorted version of the Bible as part of their strategy of dehumanization and pacification. They misinterpreted and distorted scriptural passages, such as the one from Paul's letter to Titus that says slaves should obey their masters. They supported theological perspectives that encourage submission and obedience as a virtue. And they portrayed the biblical church as a white church with a white God who favors white people as a superior race.[44]

The colonial church's genocide of the Natives and enslavement of Africans in America were done under the guise of missional gospel preaching, which has had long-lasting effects on how nonwhite Christians perceive their place within the broader church and society. One of the more prominent adverse effects is that Afro-Latino Christians perceive their social and ecclesial identity in comparison to white Christians. From such social and theological insecurities, undoubtedly rooted in the systemic racism of white normativity, emerges an indiscriminate and superficial assumption of ecclesial elements related to classical consensual Christianity. There are

---

[43]Kathy Winings, "The Challenges in Addressing White Normativity," *Applied Unificationism: A Blog of Unification Theological Seminary*, November 27, 2017, https://appliedunificationism.com/2017/11/27/the-challenges-in-addressing-white-normativity/.

[44]Joseph Barndt, *Becoming an Anti-Racist Church: Journeying Toward Wholeness* (Minneapolis: Fortress, 2011), 54.

numerous base elements of the early church that people of color will adopt, while other, more substantive and spiritually interconnected elements are shunned for being either Catholic or white. The challenge of identity politics and belonging as experienced by Afro-Latino pentecostals continues to make the recovery of classical consensual Christianity problematic. This has led to a sometimes progressive yet shallow recovery of the trappings of the Great Tradition without the substance of the Great Tradition.

Therefore, there exists within the perspective of many Afro-Latino pentecostals a limited space for how far we can travel on the road to recovery of classical Christianity before we cross the Catholic line and the phrase "this is Catholic" is uttered.

RELIGIOUS POLITICIZATION AND THE AFRO-LATINO QUEST FOR ECCLESIAL LEGITIMACY

Politicization of clerical dress. Perhaps one of the most detrimental aspects to an Afro-Latino pentecostal recovery of the Great Tradition is the appropriation, politicization, and misuse of ecclesiastical dress and rank on the part of Afro-Latino pentecostal clergy. By politicization, I mean to suggest here the process of considering ecclesiastical dress and rank as a way of understanding societal and ecclesial identification and legitimacy before considering its ecclesial, liturgical, and historical spirituality. This is done against the backdrop of socioreligious white normativity. In the struggle against whiteness and toward equality, we have lost focus on the broader church's spiritual liturgical tradition, relegating ecclesiastical dress to identity politics and feelings of legitimacy.

A practical example of this type of liturgical misuse is the contemporary appropriation and repurposing of eucharistic vestments by Afro-Latino Pentecostals. The chasuble, for example, an ecclesiastical vestment that derives "from the paenula or planeta, the outdoor cloak of both sexes in the later Graeco-Roman world," has been retained by the Orthodox Church, Anglicans, Lutherans, and Roman Catholics, worn specifically by a bishop or priest at a service where the Eucharist is celebrated.[45]

---

[45]"Chasuble," in *The Oxford Dictionary of the Christian Church*, ed. F. L. Cross and Elizabeth A. Livingstone (Oxford: Oxford University Press, 2005), 328.

Interestingly, Bishop Eric Garnes, a longstanding member of the Joint College, in his book *Protocol*, written for African American pentecostals, identifies the chasuble as a garment "adopted by the clergy in the sixth century," one that was open on the sides "for the clergy to perform their priestly duties."[46] Although Garnes goes on to speak briefly of the chasuble's origin and development, missing from his historical presentation is the description of the chasuble as a eucharistic vestment worn only within eucharistic services. One can only wonder whether resources such as these, which for whatever reason omit vital historical liturgical/sacramental descriptions, are to some extent responsible for the misuse and politicization of the chasuble within Afro-Latino pentecostal circles. Today, unfortunately, it is not uncommon to see many Afro-Latino pentecostals wearing chasubles at services where there is no Eucharist.

The pallium is another example of contemporary appropriation and politicization without consideration for ecclesial and historical tradition. This vestment, according to Herbert Norris, derives from the Greek "himation," an "oblong piece of material in its natural coloring, and of linen or wool, woven with a border and in dimensions approximately 18 feet by 6." In the first three centuries the pallium was an ordinary Roman garment used mainly by philosophers and scholars. In the middle of the fourth century, it ceased to be an ordinary garment and became "an official garment of certain high offices of the empire."[47] It was not until the middle of the fourth century and up to the sixth century when the pallium as we know it today became a shortened clerical vestment.

Although the full origin of the pallium is vague at best, according to the *Oxford Dictionary of the Christian Church* it seems to have been used by archbishops without any connection to Rome at first, yet sometime before the ninth century it became fully Roman.[48] Almost always after that the pallium was a Roman vestment, connected solely to the bishop of Rome and his authority, and was almost always conferred by the bishop of Rome

---

[46]Eric D. Garnes, *Protocol: Episcopacy, Ordination, Installation, Armorbearer, Liturgy, Eucharist* (Newark, NJ: Godzchild, 2015), 109.

[47]Herbert Norris, *Church Vestments: Their Origin and Development* (Mineola, NY: Dover, 2017), 21, 23.

[48]"Pallium," in Cross and Livingstone, *Oxford Dictionary of the Christian Church*, 1219.

to archbishops in communion with him. Even today, the pallium is recognized in the West as a "an ornament of ministers," bestowed on an archbishop by the pope as a sign of his shared authority.[49] Once again, however, as with the chasuble, it is not unusual to see Afro-Latino pentecostal clergy order a pallium to wear for what has been termed an "elevation to the office of an archbishop." Here, instead of the pallium being a sign of shared authority, which comes three months after one's ordination or appointment, it seems to be utilized as a sign or symbol of validity, rank, status, or—even worse—fashion.[50]

I am reminded of the words of E. C. Ratcliff that "liturgy, not circus, is my business."[51] It seems as though the appropriation, misuse, and politicization of vestments within segments of Afro-Latino pentecostalism has stripped them of their proper liturgical meaning, relegating them to pomp, show, and, yes, circus-stance. Any argument from Afro-Latino pentecostal clergy suggesting that these vestments must be worn in order to represent rank and therefore represent order should be a consideration of only secondary importance. As W. Jardine Grisbrooke states, "Liturgical vestments comprise a special case of ceremonial clothing and are, therefore, part of a complex pattern of communication. They serve both to express the nature of the occasion when they are worn and to distinguish the respective role and rank of each participant." For Grisbrooke, participation in the communicative liturgical role of Christian vestments should be guided by three criteria: aestheticism (beauty), theological and historical witness, and functionality.[52] Because vestments speak, the functionality of their use within the liturgy should not only clearly identify the various pastoral functions within the liturgy but should also relate to the Christian liturgical vestments of the past. Thus, any invention or innovation in the usage or construction of liturgical vestments should be discouraged.

---

[49]Norris, *Church Vestments*, 24.

[50]"Pallium," 1219.

[51]Duane L. C. M. Galles, "Whither Goes Our Liturgy?," EWTN, December 25, 1996, www.ewtn
.com/catholicism/library/whither-goes-our-liturgy-1256.

[52]W. Jardine Grisbrooke, "Vestments," in *The Study of Liturgy*, ed. Cheslyn Jones, Geoffrey Wainwright, Edward Yarnold, SJ, and Paul Bradshaw (New York: Oxford University Press, 1992), 544, 546.

Politicization of ranks. Segments of Afro-Latino pentecostalism have appropriated and politicized not only clerical dress but ecclesial ordination, appointments, and ranks as well. The church has only historically spoken of three "offices" or "orders": deacon, priest, and bishop.[53] But within segments of Afro-Latino pentecostalism the ranks or designations of archbishop, metropolitan, or overseer (away from identification with the episcopate) have been suggested to be offices as well, even though these have never been considered standalone pastoral offices or orders of the church.[54]

Another interesting contemporary development is that it is not uncommon to hear the term *elevation* being used by many Afro-Latino pentecostals to describe one's ordination or appointment to some type of office or rank. There are abundant social media graphics announcing that such and such person is being "elevated" to this office or the next. Yet, this type of thinking displays not only immersion in the social-ecclesial rat race but also what Luke Timothy Johnson describes as a type of person who sees participation in religion as access to power and success.[55] Thus, it

---

[53] An important patristic resource concerning holy orders is Ignatius of Antioch's seven letters, especially *To the Magnesians*, where he states, " I advise you, be ye zealous to do all things in godly concord, the bishop presiding after the likeness of God and the presbyters after the likeness of the council of the Apostles, with the deacons also who are most dear to me, having been entrusted with the diaconate of Jesus Christ, who was with the Father before the worlds and appeared at the end of time." Ignatius of Antioch, *Letter to the Magnesians*, ed. and trans. J. B. Lightfoot (Cambridge, OH: Christian Publishing House, 2020), 6.1. For Orthodoxy, according to Metropolitan Kallistos Ware, there are three major orders (deacon, priest, and bishop) and two minor orders (subdeacon and reader). See Ware, *The Orthodox Church*, 3rd ed. (London: Penguin Books, 2015), 290. Similarly, for the Roman Catholic tradition, Susan K. Wood, in speaking of the hierarchical and pastoral roles in *Lumen Gentium*, notes that it is "bishops, with priests and deacons as helpers, who exercise their threefold office in their service of the community, presiding in the place of God over the flock, whose shepherds they are, as teachers of doctrine, priests of sacred worship and ministers of government." See Susan K. Wood, S. C. L., *Sacramental Orders, Lex Orandi* Series (Collegeville, MN: The Liturgical Press, 2000).

[54] *The Oxford Dictionary of the Christian Church* defines "archbishop" as a title given to patriarchs in the fourth and fifth centuries and later to metropolitans and primates who had jurisdiction over an "ecclesiastical province." In the Latin Church it has almost become a title of honor for a bishop of a distinguished see. Cross, F. L., and Elizabeth A. Livingstone eds. *The Oxford Dictionary of the Christian Church*, 98. A metropolitan or an archbishop in the Greek tradition, according to Metropolitan Hilarion Alfeyev, is a rank or title that "depends not on the bishop's person, but on his episcopal see. Thus, a bishop ordained to a metropolitan see is immediately ordained with the title of metropolitan, and likewise one ordained to an archepiscopal see is ordained with the title archbishop." See Alfeyev, *Orthodox Christianity*, vol. 5, *Sacraments and Other Rites* (Yonkers, NY: St. Vladimir's Seminary Press, 2019), 168.

[55] "Interview with Professor Luke Timothy Johnson," YouTube, April 23, 2012, https://youtu.be /T28O4UI3L8Q.

seems as though for segments of Afro-Latino pentecostalism, ordination and appointments amount to ecclesial and societal success, finances, and power over others. Ordination and appointments are treated as a sort of move up in rank or status.

If the current state of affairs regarding ordination in Afro-Latino pentecostalism is to see it as an elevation, then the question must be asked, Is this type of thinking and practice affirmed or supported by the church in general? The answer to such a question is no! In fact, within the Roman Catholic tradition the term *elevation* seems to speak more to the act of elevating the consecrated host during the eucharistic anaphora than to any ministerial act of ordination, a pattern shared by the Anglican Church as well. In the Orthodox tradition the term *elevation* is connected to an actual rite, yet not as ordination itself but as a special honor or award for someone already in holy orders.

There are two Greek words that are commonly used to describe what occurs at the rite of both ordination and elevation, *cheirotonia* and *cheirothesia*. The two words share the same meaning (laying on of hands), but their usage is different. The first, *cheirotonia*, is understood to be used for the ordination of deacons, priests, and bishops, while the second, *cheirothesia*, is more commonly used for elevation to the rank of honorary positions such as archdeacon or proto-presbyter, which are given as clergy awards.[56] Also missing in the Orthodox tradition is the language of elevation for the ranks of archbishop or metropolitan. This is made clear by Metropolitan Hilarion Alfeyev, who points out that in the Russian Orthodox Church there are no rites of elevation for the ranks of archbishop or metropolitan, given that "these rites did not exist in Byzantium, since neither rank was perceived as an award." Alfeyev goes on to acknowledge, "To this day in the Greek tradition the rank of archbishop or metropolitan depends not on the bishop's person, but on his episcopal see."[57] Thus, the rank of archbishop or metropolitan in the earliest traditions was not considered an elevation and should therefore not be considered an elevation in the Afro-Latino pentecostal tradition either.

---

[56]Vladimir Latinovic and Dale Irvin, personal correspondence, August 15, 2020.
[57]Alfeyev, *Orthodox Christianity*, 5:168.

Another term appropriated, misused, and politicized within the Afro-Latino pentecostal context is that of "princes of the church." At an Afro-Latino pentecostal ordination of a bishop it is not uncommon to hear someone suggest that "a prince of the church is being made." Garnes's perspective on the matter in relation to the African American Pentecostal Episcopacy is worth quoting at length:

> Since the bishop is known as a "Prince of the Church," he is given deference by virtue of his office. The gathering into which he enters reverences his office by standing to receive his presence in the room. The attendees are expected to remain standing until the bishop grants the next directive for the assembly. He is the senior member of the royal priesthood among the clerics or those who assemble for conference. The veneration of his princely office might be greeted with a "kiss on his Episcopal ring" or an extended handshake from the bishop to the person greeting him, which is common practice here in North America. The mere privilege of being in the company of the Prince of the Church is never taken lightly and is treated as a rare privilege. Thus, every moment should be considered valuable. Any time spent in the presence of royalty is welcomed as an esteemed honor, as his gifts are shared and the infusion of their gifts into the listener's life.[58]

Three times Garnes associates the bishop with being a "prince of the church," and twice he relates the bishop to royalty. Now, I believe in respecting, honoring, and following the various offices represented as configurations to Christ, as Ignatius presents to both the Smyrnaeans and the Trallians (the bishop as Christ, priests as assembly of the apostles, and deacons as instituted by God).[59] However, has a bishop ever been known as a prince of the church and said to be due royal reverence? A simple investigation into the matter will reveal that the answer to the question is no! In fact, the term "prince of the church" describes first and foremost a clergyman who, from the third century to the Middle Ages, held in tension with his clerical rank a secular rank or position as a secular prince. In the Middle Ages Roman Catholic cardinals began to be associated with the

---

[58]Garnes, *Protocol*, 59.
[59]Ign. *Smyrn.* 8; *Trall.* 3.

term and today are still known as the princes of the church due to their proximity to the pope as advisers.[60]

How, then, can we reconcile this seemingly wide gap between how some Afro-Latino pentecostal bishops identify themselves and the reality of Roman Catholic cardinals? Recently, even Roman Catholic cardinals have been asked not to refer to themselves as princes of the church by the pontiff himself. Pope Francis, in speaking to five new cardinals, says, "They have not been called to become 'Princes of the Church' but rather to serve, with their eyes open to the realities of the 'sin of the world.'"[61] The question of the politicization and usage of the term "prince of the church" must once again be, Why? If historically it was not associated with the sole episcopacy and was later only given to cardinals in the Roman Catholic Church, and if even the pontiff of the Roman Catholic Church tells his own cardinals that they have not become princes of the church, then why do we in the Afro-Latino pentecostal context persist in wrongly using the term?

In an Afro-Latino pentecostal quest for social and ecclesial validation, recognition, and legitimacy, we have forgotten ourselves and made ourselves unsuccessful except in our own circles. In so doing we have forgotten the words of Henri Nouwen, who writes, "The way of the Christian leader is not the way of upward mobility in which our world has invested so much, but the way of downward mobility ending on the cross."[62]

Politicization of apostolic succession. The final ecclesial concept that has been heavily politicized in the Afro-Latino pentecostal context is the teaching of apostolic succession. Apostolic succession is the historic teaching of the continuation of the pastoral authority traced back to Jesus' twelve apostles. The concept is one of the most debated in contemporary ecumenical theology and heavily revolves around the notion of validity of holy orders. Within an Afro-Latino pentecostal context, the teaching of

---

[60]"Cardinal," in Cross and Livingstone, Oxford Dictionary of the Christian Church, 288; John Allen, *Conclave: The Politics, Personalities, and Process of the Next Papal Election* (New York: Doubleday, 2002), 81, 217.

[61]"Pope to New Cardinals: You're Not Called to Be 'Princes of the Church,'" *Crux*, June 28, 2017, https://cruxnow.com/vatican/2017/06/pope-new-cardinals-youre-not-called-princes-church/.

[62]Henri J. M. Nouwen, *In the Name of Jesus: Reflections on Christian Leadership* (New York: Crossroad, 2002), 37.

apostolic succession has come to emphasize legitimacy or validity of orders through a particular person's laying on of hands. Today it is not uncommon to run across a framed picture of either an apostolic succession chart that displays a line of succession from Saint Peter to the chief consecrator for the person ordained or a picture of the actual action of the laying on of hands in the service.

The majority of the time when the subject of apostolic succession is brought up in the Afro-Latino pentecostal context, its legitimacy has more to do with the popular personality of the chief consecrator and the multitude of others gathered around an episcopal ordination. Generally, segments of Afro-Latino pentecostal clergy claiming to hold apostolic succession do so by noting a connection to some Wesleyan line that was forged by some type of unverified connection John Wesley had to the Orthodox Church. This is an assertion that has never been proven and has been denounced by both Anglicans and Orthodox churches, and therefore it cannot be given any credible consideration, especially given that Wesley himself was never a bishop.

In regard to the ordination and consecration of a bishop, many Afro-Latino pentecostals follow a tradition requiring that at least three bishops (chief consecrator and two others) be present to ordain one, which can be inferred from the *Apostolic Tradition* of Hippolytus and was established at the Council of Nicaea.[63] Yet, other, more theological and historical considerations concerning the doctrine of apostolic succession seem to go unconsidered.

For example, Saint Ignatius of Antioch in his letter *To the Ephesians*, urges the believers to "Do diligence therefore to meet together more frequently for thanksgiving (Eucharist) to God and for His glory. For when ye meet together frequently, the powers of Satan are cast down."[64] This regular celebration of the Eucharist could not be disconnected from the episcopate, and vice versa, but is the "one Eucharist" itself, celebrated by the bishop with the deacons and the presbyters, which is the sign of

---

[63]See Hippolytus, *On the Apostolic Tradition*, trans. Alistar C. Stewart, Popular Patristic Series 54 (Yonkers, NY: St. Vladimir's Seminary Press, 2015) and canon 4 of the Council of Nicaea.

[64]J. B. Lightfoot, "Ignatius to the Ephesians," in *The Apostolic Fathers: The Early Christian Writings of Church Leaders who Followed Soon After the Apostles of Jesus Christ* (Cambridge, OH: Christian Publishing House, 2020), 1.13; 54.

ecclesial unity, the pattern of apostolic heavenly worship, and thus a sign of true apostolic succession.[65] Ignatius continues: "Be ye careful therefore to observe one Eucharist (for there is one flesh of our Lord Jesus Christ and one cup unto union in His blood; there is one altar, as there is one bishop, together with the presbytery and the deacons my fellow-servants), that whatsoever ye do, ye may do it after God."[66] Gregory Rogers states that for Ignatius, "The eucharistic assembly mirrors the worship of heaven, showing apostolicity to be also an eschatological reality. To be in the Eucharist with true bishops, presbyters, and deacons is to participate, in space and time, in the ministry the Apostles are now performing in heaven."[67] Apostolic lineage or succession, for Ignatius, has little to do with a simple posthumous lineage and more to do with a eucharistic and eschatological reality around the bishop. Similarly, John Zizioulas, in describing the bishop as the "president of the Eucharist" after the apostolic age, writes that celebration of the Eucharist not only became "the exclusive locus of the Bishop, but also the most vital symbol of his succession from the Apostles."[68]

This fact is worth noting because many ordinations and consecrations in some segments of Afro-Latino pentecostalism have been conducted outside a eucharistic liturgy, which is a necessity for valid orders. Most recently, some Afro-Latino pentecostal clergy, after having discovered the writings of Rogers and others concerning the conditions and forms for validity of apostolic succession, have begun to communicate the bread and the wine to only the clergy and those being ordained in the service. This action still invalidates the rite of ordination or consecration because theologically it disconnects the head (Christ) from the body (the whole church).[69]

At an even more foundational level, most Afro-Latino pentecostal clergy partaking in such politicization of the sacrament of holy orders are actually

---

[65]See Gregory Rogers, *Apostolic Succession: The Biblical Evidence, the Historical Evidence, the Twenty-First-Century Context* (Ben Lomond, CA: Conciliar, 2000), 20; Ign. *Phld.* 4.

[66]J. B. Lightfoot, "Ignatius to the Philadelphians," in *The Apostolic Fathers: The Early Christian Writings of Church Leaders who Followed Soon After the Apostles of Jesus Christ* (Cambridge, OH: Christian Publishing House, 2020), 4; 65.

[67]Rogers, *Apostolic Succession*, 20.

[68]John D. Zizioulas, *Eucharist, Bishop, Church: The Unity of the Church in the Divine Eucharist and the Bishop During the First Three Centuries* (Brookline, MA: Holy Orthodox, 2001), 65.

[69]Rogers, *Apostolic Succession*, 28.

perpetuating levels of confusion regarding a sacramental occasionalism versus a sacramental ontology or physical causality (as described in chapter two). This reality is made evident not only by the lack of a coherent, organized, or standardized liturgy for celebrating the Eucharist at services of ordination or consecration, but also by there seeming to be a major distinction in theology between the sacrament of the Eucharist and holy orders. How can most Afro-Latino pentecostal clergy believe in a sacramental ontology or physical causality of grace concerning their ordination or consecration, and yet when it comes to the sacrament of the Eucharist only believe in a sacramental occasionalism? How can one believe that through the Holy Spirit one is changed and made into a bishop, priest, or deacon, yet at the same time and within the same service not believe that by way of the same Holy Spirit the bread and wine offered changes into Christ's real body and blood?

The proof of such a way of thinking is evident in the liturgical settings for Afro-Latino pentecostal ordinations or consecrations. For most ordinations or consecrations of a bishop, for example, it is not uncommon for there to be a table designated for both episcopal appointments (vestments, ring, pectoral cross, and so on) and ordination documentation. This table is usually ornate and is put together by adjutants or overseers with the greatest amount of care and reverence. However, when it comes to the Eucharist or Communion, this table is usually an unornate, plain, 3×3 table covered with a white cloth found in some corner of the building, for which there is no reverence. On the table there usually sits one or two silver- or gold-plated Communion trays, which hold the grape juice given to the newly ordained. The Communion table is usually not given much attention or focus. The fixation on the table that holds the episcopal appointments and documentation versus the table that holds the body and blood of Christ is a practical example of how the null curriculum within Afro-Latino pentecostal teaching has contributed to the disregard for proper historical /theological liturgical setting. By taking such actions, Afro-Latino pentecostal clergy display what they believe to be most important.

Allan Doig stresses that in regard to liturgical settings, "Aspects of the setting will seem more or less appropriate to the occasion, either detracting from, or by contrast intensifying, the meaning of the rite."[70] The question for Afro-Latino pentecostal clergy who believe that they are being consecrated or ordained into apostolic succession is, Does intensifying clothes, rings, and documents properly express the meaning of the rite conducted? Given that ordination or consecration has historically usually been associated with a configuration to Christ, does the table with vestments, rings, and documents best express such a reality? Or is this reality best expressed at the table of the Lord, the table of the Eucharist, where we once again participate in the mystery of Christ's servanthood and sacrifice for the life of the world?

Another important factor for Afro-Latino pentecostal clergy to consider is that for Irenaeus of Lyons, in regard to apostolic succession, the faith of the head of each Christian community is what determines whether apostolic succession is truly present. If Ignatius looked to the eucharistic assembly around the bishop as a sign of apostolic succession, for Irenaeus it was the keeping and teaching of the apostolic faith and tradition of the church as passed on to the bishops by the apostles themselves. According to Irenaeus, "In this order, and by this succession, the ecclesiastical tradition from the apostles, and the preaching of the truth, have come down to us."[71] The preaching of historical truth along with the tradition of the apostles are two areas that are easily incorporated in the church in general, and less within the Afro-Latino pentecostal circles that claim to have apostolic succession. What many of us have come to discover is that oftentimes preaching and tradition within these segments of Afro-Latino pentecostalism have more to do with a moralistic therapeutic deist attitude and with cultural-ecclesial traditions than the preaching and traditions as passed down by the apostles to the bishops.[72] My statement in no way means to belittle or diminish the importance of cultural traditions within segments of Afro-Latino pentecostalism but

---

[70]Allan Doig, *Liturgy and Architecture: From the Early Church to the Middle Ages* (Burlington, VT: Ashgate, 2010), xxi.

[71]Irenaeus, *Against Heresies*, in *The Ante-Nicene Fathers: Translations of the Writings of the Fathers Down to A.D. 325*, ed. Alexander Roberts and James Donaldson, vol. 1 (Peabody, MA: Hendrickson Publishers, 1885), preface 2.

[72]Term developed and utilized by Christian Smith and Melina Lundquist Denton, *Soul Searching: The Religious and Spiritual Lives of American Teenagers* (New York: Oxford University Press, 2005).

rather to call for and to elicit discernment. The question must be asked, then, what preaching/teaching and what traditions of the apostles, passed on to the bishops, do Afro-Latino pentecostals who claim apostolic succession keep and teach? Questions concerning the belief in and practice of the sacraments, creedal identity, the sign of the cross, the veneration of saints, the usage of icons, the doctrine of the Trinity, and so on must be fully explored and included in any discussion concerning apostolic succession.

The politicization of apostolic succession among Afro-Latino pentecostal clergy is a recent development and breaks with earlier Afro-Latino pentecostal thinking. Neither Charles Mason nor William Seymour expressly claimed to have apostolic succession, though they ordained bishops using a recognizable historical rite and kept many of the liturgical practices borrowed from the Methodist and Anglican traditions. Both men seemed content with being called to and producing apostolic works, a thought that current Afro-Latino pentecostal clergy should embrace over against worrying solely about apostolic succession.

Given all this, imagine what it would be like for an Afro-Latino pentecostal cleric who knew nothing of the teaching or the traditions of the Fathers, nor was sacramental in any way, to attend an ecumenical function hosted by Roman Catholics dressed in a chasuble and a pallium. Would that not be akin to nonmilitary personnel attending a military function dressed in a uniform covered with medals not only unearned but also not properly used or understood? This type of ecclesial appropriation or repurposing demonstrates the very thin line Afro-Latino pentecostals draw when recovering elements of the Great Tradition. The question must be asked, Are vestments in the Afro-Latino pentecostal church uniforms and fashion statements devoid of true pastoral, historic, spiritual representation? Do Afro-Latino pentecostals care about the historic spirituality connected to vestments, or do vestments merely represent status and decorum? Even more pressing, Do Afro-Latino pentecostals care for the poor ecumenical witness this type of careless reappropriation brings about?

Come On, Man!

As a way of providing a very practical example of how the politicization mentioned above operates, I share the following true experience, which I have edited some to protect those involved.

Some years ago, as I was traveling back home from a conference where I had been invited to speak, I met a young African American bishop from one of the pentecostal "reformations" at the airport. It has been my experience that the word *reformation* has been used particularly in the Joint College context to mean "jurisdictions," although *jurisdiction* and *reformation* have completely distinct and separate historical, ecclesial, and theological meanings. But in any case, this young bishop was dressed in all-black clerics (civic attire). His episcopal ring was enormous and had a huge amethyst stone with diamonds all around it. I could not see his pectoral cross, but I assumed that it might have been as decorated as his ring. I must admit, he did have a certain swag about him. As he sat down next to me, we locked eyes, exchanged pleasantries, and began a conversation. Now, anybody who knows me knows that for years I have preferred to travel comfortably. I do not have a habit of dressing up at all during flights unless I am going right into a conference or preaching engagement. This day, just like so many times before, I was dressed in jeans, sneakers, and a black sports pullover (which just happens to be one of my favorites). After a while of conversing, the young bishop began to tell me about his ministry, his episcopacy, religious connections, and churches across the country.

I asked about his formation and education (I am always interested in knowing), and he answered by mentioning several conferences or events he had attended, and several books he had read. By this time, it was quite noticeable to me that he had no real classical episcopal training of any kind, but I dismissed the thought as quickly as it came, attempting not to be so judgmental of other people's processes. Just then, as he began to tell me of his understanding of apostolic succession and protocol, a woman across from us suddenly clutched her chest and slumped to the ground. A few passengers around us ran to her aid, and someone yelled, "Call the police!" The woman, seemingly in pain, was holding her chest with her hand, which had her crucifix in it. She looked directly at the one person at the gate with a collar on and began to mumble words toward the bishop. Her voice must have been heard by the gentleman that was closest to her because he looked up at the bishop and said, "Prayer! Last rites!" The bishop sitting next to me looked at me as if he were a deer caught in headlights—frozen. As I looked at his face of bewilderment, it was all too clear to me that he did not know what to do.

I went to her and, after identifying myself as a non–Roman Catholic bishop, began my prayer, reciting the Apostles' Creed first. By the end of the creed the paramedics showed up and took her away, and the whole ordeal was over as quickly as it began. I returned to my seat next to the bishop, who was silent and seemed to be embarrassed. I was angry and frustrated.

The point of this story is not to embarrass, humiliate, or call out fellow clergy members who lack a particular type of training but to bring about an awareness of the greater issue at stake. The story should cause pause and greater reflection concerning the very real public expectations that come with adopting a certain public dress or uniform. Have Afro-Latino pentecostal clergy been taught the ecumenical implications of public ecclesial garb so as to be able to deal with public emergencies? Whether a young African American pentecostal bishop at an airport or an older Latino pentecostal bishop dressed in a purple chasuble at a Bible study where there is no Eucharist, it seems to me as though some segments of an Afro-Latino pentecostalism are guilty of developing pentecostal clergy who are unable to interact with the various Christian traditions with the most basic of understandings. My comments stem not from my yearning to criticize but from my passion for the formation of African Americans and Latin@s, especially as it relates to recovering the treasures of the Great Tradition. How long will we allow our clergy to wear collars and colors without knowing councils and creeds, wear flashy crosses without foundational catechism, wear big rings without a proper liturgical understanding of rituals, wear vestments without true vows, and believe in apostolic succession but be unable to recall any of the "assumed" historical antecedents (bishops, theologians, doctors)?

Now, someone might argue, "Well, last rites are Catholic, and he wasn't a Catholic priest or bishop." Yes, an argument can be made regarding the

Council of Florence in 1439, where the Roman Catholic Church called the rite of anointing "extreme unction" and said it was to be administered to its members only in the face of death as a final step of penance. This understanding, however, was changed after Vatican II, when a more relaxed approach was considered that saw the sacrament of anointing regain its proper singular place.[73] The practice of anointing the sick and dying, according to Everett Ferguson, "was first identified as a sacrament in the ninth century and numbered among the seven sacraments by Peter Lombard in the twelfth."[74] This means not only that it has a biblical basis, found in James 5:14-15, but also that it was believed and practiced by the church before the Great Schism of 1054, placing it, at least in paleo-orthodox thinking, within the framework of consensual ecclesial recovery.

Aside from all of the minutiae concerning who can and cannot administer and who can receive last rites in the Roman tradition, there should have at least been a basic impulse on the part of the young bishop to join the woman in a word of prayer.[75] This example, although brief, should cause us to question the formational process of our Afro-Latino pentecostal brothers and sisters who go out into the world making a very public statement by dressing in clerical attire without knowing the various biblical and historical rites that accompany such dress.

MIMICRY: MOCKERY OR MENACE?

To what extent does the Afro-Latino pentecostal misappropriation of liturgical trappings cause more harm than good? The politicization of ranks, dress, and authority, as well as the conversation regarding "reformations," legitimacy, and validation that takes place within segments of Afro-Latino pentecostal leadership, brings to mind Homi Bhabha's concept of mimicry. Segments of Afro-Latino pentecostalism recovering base elements of the Great Tradition should seriously consider this concept.

---

[73]See Andrew Davison, "Anointing," in *Why Sacraments* (London: SPCK, 2013), 120-28.

[74]Everett Ferguson, "Sacraments in the Pre-Nicene Period," in *The Oxford Handbook of Sacramental Theology*, ed. Hans Boersma and Matthew Levering (New York: Oxford University Press, 2015), 138.

[75]"Catechism of the Catholic Church" (Vatican City: Vatican Press, 1993), 1514-16, www.vatican .va/archive/ENG0015/__P4L.HTM.

In his well-circulated article "Of Mimicry and Man: The Ambivalence of Colonial Discourse," Bhabha uses Jacques Lacan's definition of mimicry as "revealing something in so far as it is distinct from what might be called an itself that is behind. The effect of mimicry is camouflage. . . . It is not a question of harmonizing with the background, but against a mottled background, of becoming mottled—exactly like the technique of camouflage practiced in human warfare." Within the context of colonialism, mimicry is the process of "desire for a reformed, recognizable Other, as a subject of a difference that is almost the same but not quite." Mimicry is inclusive of double articulation of reform, regulation, and discipline, which "appropriates the Other as it visualizes power." This double articulation can result in mimicry as mockery or mimicry as menace inasmuch as it displays a "partial representation," which disrupts authority or authenticity.[76]

The politicization of rank, dress, and legitimacy within segments of Afro-Latino pentecostalism is at best a partial representation of the authentic because it comes without the recovery of authentic historic spirituality (sacraments, liturgical theology, and tradition). If this is true, how much of our mimicry has become a mockery of the sacred and a menace to the spiritual and ecumenical? Does this mimicry stem from the unconscious but ongoing effects of slavery, colonization, and racism? Who and what forms the backdrop against which our striving for legitimacy and validation is set up? Furthermore, through what biblical, historical, or cultural lens are pentecostals who are recovering base elements of the Great Tradition filtering the issues present in their global cities, and how is that influencing their formation? I have found that, more often than not, our Afro-Latino pentecostal clerics are being formed by processes disconnected from both an early African Christian narrative and a Native Indian/ Latino contextualization of the same.

The predominantly European retelling and interpretation of the historic Christianity found among many of our Afro-Latino churches has been the main backdrop against which we are all now attempting to fit in. In fact, these frameworks or perspectives that are mimicked without liturgical or

---

[76]Homi Bhabha, "Of Mimicry and Man: The Ambivalence of Colonial Discourse," *October* 28 (1984): 126, 129.

sacramental authenticity have indeed become the new boats used in a post-modern Middle Passage that continues to attempt to disconnect people of color from their contextualized or cultural Christian identity and instead connects them to a nationalized American spirituality. Antipas Harris tells a story about how, when the curse of Shem was under consideration at a Bible study, someone stated that "black people have reason to thank God for slavery because he used slavery to deliver black people from the savagery of Africa and introduce them to Jesus."[77] History has shown us that there are those of us who continue to be punished for causing uprisings along the way, and there are also those of us who have made up our minds to get off these ideological boats altogether.

EARLY AFRICAN CHRISTIANITY

As an alternative to the mostly white European framework from which Afro-Latino pentecostals work, a recovery of early African Christianity could help to remedy the memory gap when it comes to the recovery of the Great Tradition. Esau McCaulley suggests that Luke can be a Gospel writer for Black Christians. McCaulley compares Luke's concern for Theophilus's correct understanding of the things he has been taught about Jesus (among alternative Jesus narratives) with the conversion process of enslaved African Americans at the hands of white slave owners. The question is "whether the Christianity that the enslaved were taught was indeed the Christianity of the Bible."[78]

People of color in general, but for the sake of this work Afro-Latino pentecostals in particular, continue to struggle with the dangers of believing alternative European narratives pertaining to Christian spirituality. As already stated above, there continues to exist a deeply suspicious Catholo-phobia and thus a "whiteophobia" on the part of Afro-Latino pentecostals regarding historic Christian spirituality. However, just as Luke wrote to Theophilus to provide him with an "orderly account" of events (Lk 1:1 NRSV), there is a strong movement toward the recovery of early

---

[77]Harris, *Is Christianity the White Man's Religion?*, 95.
[78]Esau McCaulley, *Reading While Black: African American Biblical Interpretation as an Exercise in Hope* (Downers Grove, IL: IVP Academic, 2020), 78.

African Christianity as a corrective to an ahistorical European telling not only of the gospel but also of church history.

The lapse in memory on the part of Afro-Latino Christians in regard to early African Christian identity and spirituality is not only because of the dominant European retelling of the gospel but also because of the gap in space and time from the coast of western Africa then to North America now. The claim that the Africans who were taken from the western shores had no understanding of the Christian God has always been challenging to me, seeing as though it is estimated that half or more of those taken did not survive the Middle Passage. My question was always, How are we to know for sure? Vince Bantu has answered this question, showing that Christianity did indeed exist on the shores of west Africa before the trans-atlantic slave trade of the 1500s, a discovery that gives pause to critics who say that Christianity is the "white man's religion or that the white man brought Christianity to Africans."[79]

I am often asked, Why should Black or brown Christians study early African Christianity? How would doing so inform being a Black or brown Christian in America? It seems to me that the question itself not only displays the ongoing concern for Black and brown bodies in North America but also exhibits a continual racial suspicion of historic Christianity. Dwight Hopkins suggests that slave and ex-slave narratives "provide foundational elements for the creation of a constructive black theology of liberation." These narratives, however, cannot lay passive but must "compel black theology to deepen further its reliance on indigenous resources in the African American church and community, thereby commanding black theology to cut loose its stammering tongue."[80] To what extent, then, can early African Christian resources re-unearthed by Bantu, Thomas Oden, David Wilhite, and others be considered indigenous to the African American religious experience? To what extent can Afro-Latino pente-costals in particular reclaim this reality? To do so would be to live up to the

---

[79]Vince Bantu, *The Bisrat: Apologetics in African Terms* (Jude 3 Project, 2020), https://jude3project .org/new-products/bisrat.

[80]Dwight N. Hopkins and George Cummings, *Cut Loose Your Stammering Tongue: Black Theology in the Slave Narrative* (Maryknoll, NY: Orbis Books, 1991), xv-xvi.

words of Cardinal Joseph-Albert Malula of Zaire: "In the past, foreign missionaries Christianized Africa. Today the Christians of Africa are invited
to Africanize Christianity."[81]

For Afro-Latino pentecostals looking to recover classical consensual
orthodoxy, it is neither prudent nor practical to look solely to Eurocentric
models of Christian orthodoxy. For Oden, to exclude early African
Christian resources from the process of an orthodox formation resembles
a wise owl (representing philosophy) with blinders on that can only fly
after the day is done (reality).[82] The analogy is that of philosophical inquiry,
which never took care to fly over Africa.

African Christian scholarship has helped debunk far-fetched and false
Eurocentric notions of Christian missional efforts embedded within colonialism and slavery. The outrageous claim that slavery as an institution
brought Christianity to the heathen from across the ocean has been prob-
lematized once again, not only by showing that Christianity did indeed
exist beforehand, as mentioned above, but also by establishing African
Christian identity within the patristic era, which predates modern colonialism. This early African orthodoxy, according to Oden, is "the form of
classic Christian consensual teaching that was first planted in Africa by
Africans from Mark to Clement to Tertullian to Cyprian to Augustine to
Cyril the Great—all African born, all affirming the same core faith."[83]
Oden ventures to show that the Western Christian mind benefits from
learning how African thinkers shaped dogma and spiritual formation as
well as how they provided a pattern for the early ecumenical councils.[84]
While an exaggerated Christian Afrocentrism must be rejected as historically imbalanced, the sometimes forgotten story of Christian thought as
developed in Africa has helped Afro-Latino pentecostals look beyond
white normativity in their recovery of classical consensual orthodoxy. This

---

[81]Quoted in Achille Mbembe, "Rome and the African Churches," *Pro Mundi Vita Dossiers* 2-3
(1986): 30.

[82]Thomas C. Oden, *The Rebirth of African Orthodoxy: Return to Foundations* (Nashville: Abingdon,
2016), 25.

[83]Oden, *Rebirth of African Orthodoxy*, 11.

[84]Thomas C. Oden, *How Africa Shaped the Christian Mind: Rediscovering the African Seedbed of Western
Christianity* (Downers Grove, IL: InterVarsity Press, 2007), 43. See also Oden, *Early Libyan Christianity: Uncovering a North African Tradition* (Downers Grove: IVP Academic, 2011).

recovery, however, cannot be limited to Oden's reconstruction, which mainly posits Roman and Byzantine Christian traditions as platforms for recovery, but must also be inclusive of African, Asian, and Middle Eastern non-Chalcedonian churches as well. The Coptic, Syrian, and Asian Orthodox churches can provide Afro-Latinos with a more recognizable path toward the recovery of the Great Tradition.[85]

Writings concerning early African Christian thought have been instrumental in redirecting the Afro-Latino pentecostal mind toward the recovery of classical consensual thinking, and the rediscovery of Afro-Latino saints and martyrs has provided incarnational examples of holy living. Ascetic monks such as Moses the Black along with Spanish saints such as Saint Martin de Porres have aided Afro-Latino pentecostals in placing their cultural identity in interplay with orthodox practice and belief.

CONCLUSION

The most base elements of the Great Tradition that most Afro-Latino pentecostals I encounter are recovering have less to do with creedal adherence or sacramental spirituality and more to do with social-ecclesial uniformity, racial dignity, and validation. These attempts at recovery are practical and include innovative liturgical rituals. Some of these efforts to gain and convey a sense of ecclesial and social validation can be seen as a continuing disposition of the greater "invisible institution" (i.e., slave religion), which empowered and gave hope to black preachers and black theology, as Albert Raboteau's *Slave Religion* masterfully portrays.[86] Much of what has been learned in regard to ecclesial dress and designation, however, can also be connected to various African American ecclesial developments after Reconstruction, when Anglicanism and Methodism provided new organizational identity for African Americans before the Azusa Street revival of 1906.[87]

Contemporary Afro-Latino pentecostals must ask themselves whether an ingrained Catholo-phobia that perceives traditional forms of the faith

---

[85]Here again, anyone looking to further their reflection on this matter should read Bantu's treatment of the matter in *A Multitude of All Peoples*.

[86]Albert J. Raboteau, *Slave Religion: The "Invisible Institution" in the Antebellum South* (New York: Oxford University Press, 2004).

[87]This fact is considered by Lincoln and Mamiya, *Black Church*, and Giggie, *After Redemption*.

as white supremacy, along with a basic yearning for ecclesial dignity, will keep Afro-Latino pentecostals from recovering more than superficial elements of classical consensual orthodoxy. Will we continue in mimicry that ends in religious mockery and social-ecclesial menace? These hurdles of identity politics and suspicion can only be overcome by way of early Christian African–oriented resources, contextual formational programs, and religious educational philosophies that encourage Afro-Latino pentecostals to grasp and recover the Great Tradition without losing their pentecostal identity and spirituality.

5

AN ECUMENISM OF THE SPIRIT

THE TWENTY-FIRST CENTURY is witnessing a surge in ecumenical experience and expression. These experiences and expressions are fresh and diverse, and they are being developed by the Holy Spirit through a grassroots dynamic now inclusive of pentecostals recovering the Great Tradition. This new ecumenism differs from the old ecumenical dialogue of the twentieth century in that, while the old focused on the political and missional efforts of the institutional church to achieve some type of visible unity, the new ecumenism is interested in proving the already-existing unity occurring between Christians on a daily basis. The new ecumenism is being built on ecclesial expressions with an already-established experiential and dialectical ecumenism with the classical, ancient Christian witness, practiced and believed without the permission of religious bureaucrats. It comes to the present ecumenical context already informed and is unified with the saints and sacraments of old, even if it is not allowed to be unified with the established churches they represent. While the old ecumenism continues to insist on dialogue with existing heads of Christian traditions as its principal methodological approach toward unity, the new looks to have an experience before engaging in dialogue and takes into account emerging ecclesial communities as conversation partners.

A Pentecostal orthodox expression is one of the major incubators producing ecclesiological developments that are intentionally based on and open to grassroots movement of the Holy Spirit. This movement can be properly called an "ecumenism of the Spirit." As I will explain in this chapter, it stands in contrast to the "spiritual ecumenism" of the modern era.

SPIRITUAL ECUMENISM

The old, twentieth-century ecumenism has both bureaucratic and public political leanings. According to Dale Irvin, this old ecumenism "assumed unifying models of authority (monarchical or republican) exercised by heads of communion that were modeled on the political apparatus of the state for governance." It operated and continues to operate under "a complex imperial memory that began with Constantine." From this perspective, the goal of ecumenism is to recover the organizational expression of institutional unity and public recognition that supposedly existed in the church from the fourth century until the Reformation. In this respect, the old ecumenism continues to be haunted by the specter of Emperor Constantine the Great.[1]

Similarly, for Thomas Oden, "The old ecumenism brought institutions together to agree on high-sounding documents and bold-sounding revolutionary public-policy proposals."[2] It began with an ecclesial/political focus and sought to model public unity among Christians through the same Constantinian measures taken in the fourth century. This type of old ecumenism imagined

> that the visible unity will be accomplished by getting institutions and groups to agree with each other, verbally and formally, even if reduced to the lowest common nondoctrinal denominator, especially in supposed political acts that give the appearance of great prophetic courage, though they are carried out with a steady eye toward favorable journalistic reporting.[3]

Since the driving impetus for the old ecumenical movement is the public display of ecclesial/political unity, the institutional monarchs of each church take primary responsibility for striving to achieve this unity.

---

[1] Dale T. Irvin, "Specters of a New Ecumenism: In Search of a Church Out of Joint," in *Religion, Authority, and the State: From Constantine to the Contemporary World*, ed. Leo D. Lefebure (New York: Palgrave Macmillan, 2016), 1, 13.

[2] Thomas C. Oden, *The Rebirth of Orthodoxy: Signs of New Life in Christianity* (New York: HarperCollins, 2003), 58.

[3] Oden, *Rebirth of Orthodoxy*, 58.

There is no better identifying marker for this old ecumenism than Cardinal Walter Kasper's "spiritual ecumenism." For Kasper, "Spiritual ecumenism finds its expression in the public and private prayer for the unity of Christians."[4] Some argue spiritual ecumenism is influenced primarily by the Second Vatican Council, which affirmed that the ecumenical movement "has been brought about under the inspiring grace of the Holy Spirit."[5] This brand of ecumenism presents believers with three distinct challenges. First, although beneficial, a spiritual ecumenism is too often limited to a focus on public prayer for institutional Christian unity, and as such does not attend fully to the promptings of the Spirit as both a challenging and unifying presence in the lives of Christians and Christian communities. The old ecumenism is only open to the Spirit insofar as the Spirit affirms, further develops, and brings together in greater visible unity the existing ecclesial structures. It does not attend to and may even be said to turn away from the possibility that the Spirit is calling for the reshaping and refashioning of existing ecclesial structures.

Second, spiritual ecumenism gives a preeminent place to the prayers of the people instead of the ecumenical prayer of Jesus as found in John 17, which can be viewed as a call to all Christians to go beyond a focus on the institutional church and strive to contribute to a unified effort to be an effective gospel witness within the world. Finally, the old ecumenism is seen as "a spiritual process, carried out in faithful obedience to the Father, following the will of Christ, under the guidance of the Holy Spirit." Such obedient action taken by believers under the guidance of the Holy Spirit is "the soul of the whole ecumenical movement."[6] In the old ecumenism, obedient human action takes precedence over a present acting divinity and an openness to recognizing how the Holy Spirit could lead us beyond existing ecclesial structures to embrace new ways of being the people of God.

---

[4] Cardinal Walter Kasper, *A Handbook of Spiritual Ecumenism* (New York: New City Press, 2007), 10.
[5] Second Vatican Council, *Unitatis redintegratio*, 1964, n. 1.
[6] Kasper, *Spiritual Ecumenism*, 11.

An Ecumenism of the Spirit

If the old ecumenism, as articulated by Kasper, can be called "spiritual ecumenism," then the new ecumenism taking place within postmodernity can be called an "ecumenism of the Spirit." This new ecumenism cannot discount the older ecumenism and to a large extent must build on its already-established structures even as it strives to move beyond it. To use Irvin's language, which follows Robert Gardiner, an ecumenism of the Spirit is "an inexpedient ecumenism, or the ecumenism of the inexpedient." While the old ecumenism is interested in negotiated interinstitutional public unity, the new ecumenism "continuously blurs the lines between unity and mission, or church and world. It is far more indeterminate in its understanding of authority that is exercised in both foundational and non-foundational ways."[7]

Instead of following the nation-state model as an organizing principle, a new ecumenism resembles translocal and transnational networks, which "follow the flow of markets as they cross national boundaries." Whereas in the old ecumenism one could only be and represent one thing; the new ecumenism is "emergent, convergent, charismatic, pentecostal, missional, evangelical, constructive" and allows for participation in more than one Christian tradition.[8] It is inclusive of women and people of color as principal players within countermovements that have opposed most of the old political ecumenism. The new ecumenism does not lead such movements to identify themselves as anything other than ecclesial bodies within the one, holy, catholic, and apostolic church, and because of their unconstrained openness to being led by the Spirit, Pentecostal Orthodox bodies such as the Union of Charismatic Orthodox Churches are increasingly being looked at as contributors to a new, visible ecumenism.

Recognizing the need for these kinds of ecclesial communities, the *Princeton Proposal for Christian Unity*, published in 2003, states, "It is our conviction that those unconstrained by bureaucratic roles and free from the limitations of official leadership have a distinctive call to the service of

---

[7]Irvin, "Specters of a New Ecumenism," 1, 15.
[8]Irvin, "Specters of a New Ecumenism," 1, 17.

unity." These convergent, charismatic, ecclesial communities are emerging forms of a new and yet historical (that is, historically grounded) ecclesial ecumenism. They contribute to ecclesial developments while having no official standing, and thus, in the words of the *Princeton Proposal*, have "greater freedom for new initiatives."[9]

Oden, recognizing how the Spirit is made manifest through these new ecclesial communities, identifies them as institutional instruments. He purposefully shies away from talking about institutional organizations, preferring to place institutions in the hands of the Spirit as instruments. These institutional instruments bring about unity all around the world and can be seen in "believing Christians in every communion, but also in international ministries that express Christian unity concretely and pragmatically, transcending denominational boundaries." Oden continues to assert, "This uniting work of the Holy Spirit is taking form on a breathtaking world scale, and yet it is manifested primarily in quiet and inconspicuous ways in local churches, parachurch ministries, and unobtrusive grassroots missions."[10]

Here we can sharpen the analysis to posit the difference between an ecumenism of the Spirit and spiritual ecumenism on levels of both intentionality and action. An ecumenism of the Spirit is the Spirit's work, and it can be mostly seen outside the traditional religious structures (World Council of Churches, apostolic succession, and so on), while spiritual ecumenism is the work of Christians within mostly authoritative structures, albeit carried out under the guidance and grace of the Spirit. The two are not disconnected, as already expressed above. Spiritual ecumenism, which is the responsibility of every Christian, in no uncertain terms expresses the holistic (ecumenical) work of the Spirit. Ecumenism of the Spirit is the intentional work of the Spirit at a grassroots level producing ecclesiological developments that bring cause for a greater manifestation of visible unity. But those developments of spiritual ecumenism are more properly identified as effects of the ecumenism of the Spirit.

---

[9] Carl E. Braaten and Robert W. Jenson, *In One Body Through the Cross: The Princeton Proposal for Christian Unity* (Grand Rapids, MI: Eerdmans, 2003), 51.

[10] Oden, *Rebirth of Orthodoxy*, 63, 57.

Key to understanding these ecclesiological developments brought on by an ecumenism of the Spirit is the Spirit's intentional action, as stated above, in creating amalgamated ecclesial communities. As a master teacher practicing a gestalt method, the leading and guiding Spirit pulls from diverse streams of the Christian tradition, bringing men and women together in order to form new ecclesial communities that take on the whole of Christian tradition and treasures as their heritage. Through a practical religious-educational dynamic combined with a mystical yearning for knowledge concerning the Great Tradition, the Spirit provides a second language construct, aligning theological orthodoxy and the liturgical /sacramental with Pentecostal and evangelical belief systems. Pentecostals are introduced to the church's liturgy and sacraments, while others of a more liturgical or sacramental bent are introduced to the Spirit's ecstatic manifestations and a more word-oriented perspective. The result is that through an ecumenism of the Spirit pentecostal Christians are being introduced to treasures old and new, developing a deep love for the fullness of ecclesiastical life and a more balanced stewardship of belief and practice.

Because a new ecumenism "is not headquartered in any particular bureaucracy or establishment but is as diffuse as is the uniting work of the Holy Spirit," it presents the world with forms of church unity that go far beyond the human attempts of the old spiritual ecumenism.[11] Oden identifies this new ecumenism as an older, classical Christian ecumenism birthed in the Jerusalem Council (AD 46). It is Spirit-led, grassroots, nonhierarchical, and grounded on ancient ecumenical teaching.[12] In giving the Spirit homage for his primary role within a new ecumenism, Oden states:

> Rather, what the Holy Spirit is doing in the world today is something very different from creating institutional unity through negotiation or strategic agreement or talk. The Spirit is eliciting faith. Faith is eliciting works of love. Those whose faith is active in love recognize each other as the family of God. This recognition is itself a gift of the Holy Spirit. While the old liberal

---

[11]Oden, *Rebirth of Orthodoxy*, 57.
[12]Thomas C. Oden, *Turning Around the Mainline: How Renewal Movements Are Changing the Church* (Grand Rapids, MI: Baker, 2006), 62.

ecumenists want to talk, talk, talk, and talk some more, these believers want to experience behavior-transforming personal faith in Jesus Christ as Lord.[13]

Carl E. Braaten, reflecting on the same foundational works of love and faith Oden mentions, notes, "There is an ecumenism born of the flesh of the ecclesiastical politics that shaves truth for the sake of harmony, and there is an ecumenism born of the Spirit that unites people at the grassroots in faith, hope, and love."[14] The role of dialogue, primary in the old spiritual ecumenism, seems to have become secondary in an ecumenism of the Spirit. The primary place in ecumenical relationships is now occupied by experiences that produce faith and works of love. In fact, for Oden the term *dialogue* has come to define the old liberal ecumenists who just want to talk, "with the intent of co-opting the faithful for political actions." Oden contends that in the hands of the old ecumenism, "dialogue itself has often become an instrument of manipulation."[15]

Oden's argument not only highlights how the new ecumenism of the Spirit differs from the old spiritual ecumenism in various ways but also sets the working dynamics for one of Pentecostal orthodoxy's main contributions to ecumenism, namely, its emphasis on the experience of love through the baptism in the Holy Spirit.

Now that I have established some of the ways an ecumenism of the Spirit differs from spiritual ecumenism, I can, in true dialectical form, examine three foundational elements concerning a Pentecostal orthodoxy and ecumenism. First, while the old ecumenism is said to have been birthed from the nineteenth-century missionary movement, to what extent can it be said that the experiential dynamic in an ecumenism of the Spirit was birthed from the twentieth-century Pentecostal movement? Second, how and why are adherents of a Pentecostal orthodoxy so comfortable with the writings of the Fathers, liturgical worship, and sacramental theology? Last, what are some of the contributions a Pentecostal orthodoxy can make to Pentecostal–Roman Catholic /Orthodox dialogues?

---

[13]Oden, *Turning Around the Mainline*, 63.
[14]Carl E. Braaten, *Mother Church: Ecclesiology and Ecumenism* (Minneapolis: Fortress, 1998), 5.
[15]Oden, *Turning Around the Mainline*, 46.

AN ECUMENISM OF THE SPIRIT AND EARLY
PENTECOSTAL BONDS OF LOVE

If there is anything within early Pentecostal thinking that a Pentecostal orthodoxy can draw from regarding Christian unity, it would be its emphasis on love as a sign of the experience of baptism in the Holy Spirit. An ecumenism of the Spirit becomes a simple category, looking to recapture early twentieth-century Pentecostal thinking concerning Christian unity as useful in resetting a new foundational platform for future ecumenical interaction.

For Douglas Jacobsen, early Pentecostal leaders such as Richard Spurling and David Myland represent strong proponents of Christian unity, while Seymour represents a more moderate proponent.[16] Wolfgang Vondey, however, sees Spurling's ecumenical use of the term "Christian union," and Myland's "oneness" or "one-accordness" perspective in the Latter Rain writings, as one with Seymour's understanding of Pentecostalism as a restorationist movement.[17] For Seymour, love as a "fundamental trait" or "evidence" of the baptism of the Holy Spirit is connected to his ecumenical sensitivity.[18] Irvin sees Seymour's ecumenical, pastoral vision of love and service "manifested in the interracial and transcultural experience of worship in the Spirit, with the gifts of tongues playing an important (but not exclusive) role as a biblical sign of the fullness of the human community."[19] Through Seymour and other early Pentecostal leaders alike, the restorationist movement emphasized a unifying ecumenism of love through the baptism in the Holy Spirit, which (unlike creeds and confessions, which divided believers) helped to heal ecclesial divisions.[20]

In the baptismal experience of the Spirit of love held by early Pentecostals, "no national identity, language or culture was to be excluded in

---

[16]Douglas Jacobsen, "The Ambivalent Ecumenical Impulse in Early Pentecostal Theology," in *Pentecostalism and Christian Unity: Ecumenical Documents and Critical Assessments,* ed. Wolfgang Vondey (Eugene, OR: Pickwick, 2010), 4-7.

[17]See Jacobsen, "Ambivalent Ecumenical Impulse," 7-10; see also Wolfgang Vondey, "Pentecostalism and Ecumenism," in *The Cambridge Companion to Pentecostalism,* ed. Cecil M. Robeck and Amos Yong (New York: Cambridge University Press, 2014), 274.

[18]Jacobsen, "Ambivalent Ecumenical Impulse," 7-10; Vondey, "Pentecostalism and Ecumenism," 274.

[19]Dale Irvin, "Drawing All Together in One Bond of Love: The Ecumenical Vision of William Seymour and the Azusa Street Revival," *Journal of Pentecostal Theology* 3, no. 6 (1995): 32.

[20]Irvin, "Drawing All Together," 39.

God's new Pentecostal movement."[21] This same baptism of love confronted gender inequality, racism, and social and economic class distinctions, considering them nothing more than a mere continuation of human creedal formulas.

For early Pentecostals such as Seymour, tongues were a secondary sign that spoke of the inward acceptance of the "other" brought on by love. Irvin, speaking of the same, concludes, "The Pentecostal theology of 'otherness' of tongues goes beyond the Protestant theologies of vernacular worship, beyond catholic inclusion achieved through the unity of a creed. It represents a more radical moment of transcendence that marks a place for all peoples of the earth, in their own terms, in their own tongues."[22]

A Pentecostal orthodoxy involved in an ecumenism of the Spirit sees both areas mentioned by Irvin—"Protestant vernacular worship" and "catholic creeds"—come together in a new, holistic experience that looks not only to the past to recover its ecumenical footing but to the future in order to face contemporary ecumenical challenges. As Vondey eloquently puts it, "Contemporary pentecostalism is undergoing a transformational renewal on a global level that has taken the movement to the boundaries of its own identity by shifting focus away from issues relating to the major emphases of classical Pentecostalism and toward a global theological agenda that is of broad ecumenical significance."[23]

ANAMNESIS AS AGENT OF ECUMENISM

In speaking of a new ecumenism and Christian truths, Oden asks, "How do such varied Christians find inspiration and common faith within this joint effort?" His response is that the texts on which classical Christianity is grounded are "intrinsically and obviously ecumenical, undeniably Catholic in their cultural range."[24] For Oden, all Christian traditions have an equal right to appeal to the earliest Spirit-led writings of historic Christianity, inclusive of Scripture as well as patristic writings.

---

[21]Irvin, "Drawing All Together," 45.
[22]Irvin, "Drawing All Together," 51.
[23]Vondey, "Pentecostalism and Ecumenism," 286.
[24]Oden, *Rebirth of Orthodoxy*, 64.

As a pentecostal who has recovered both the spiritual and theological riches of the Great Tradition, I am frequently asked a similar
question: "How are you so comfortable teaching the Fathers, celebrating the Eucharist weekly, or following the liturgical calendar?"—
especially since I grew up in a tradition where all of the above was
virtually nonexistent. If an ecumenism of the Spirit, as Oden has suggested, is a grassroots movement birthing ecclesiological developments
(such as a Pentecostal orthodoxy) that base their beliefs on conciliar
and consensual Christianity, then through what means do people
within their congregations come to know orthodox truths? After many
years of development, I have come to believe that an ecumenism of the
Spirit operates through a kind of experiential anamnesis that aids believers who have been historically disconnected from the Great Tradition in recovering its riches.

Almost exclusively, to speak of anamnesis, or recollection, is to speak of
the Christian understanding of the death, resurrection, and ascension of
Jesus made manifest to us through the Eucharist. It is the "do this in remembrance of me" phrase that shows up in 1 Corinthians 11 and in our
anaphoric eucharistic prayers after the words of institution.[25] There has
been some debate as to whether this belief stems from the Jewish custom
registered in Exodus 12–13, where, in answer to a son who questions how
the Lord delivered Israel, the father is to respond, "By strength of hand the
LORD brought us out of Egypt" (Ex 13:14). This answer, throughout generations to the present, is always to be given not only in the affirmative but
also in historic participation through the use of the pronoun *us*.

The earliest Christian communities understood the word *remembrance*
differently from Western postmodern Christians. In speaking of anamnesis
and the Eucharist, Saint John Chrysostom states that in offering the Eucharist as sacrifice, "we always offer the same, not one sheep now and to-
morrow another, but always the same thing: so that the sacrifice is one.
And yet by this reasoning, since the offering is made in many places, are
there many Christs? But Christ is one everywhere, being complete here

---

[25]"Anamnesis," in *The Oxford Dictionary of the Christian Church*, ed. F. L. Cross and Elizabeth A. Livingstone (Oxford: Oxford University Press, 2005), 57.

and complete there also, one Body."[26] Jean Danielou's reading of Chrysostom leads him to conclude that the "power of the anamnesis" is found in making the resurrected Christ present not in memory but in reality. For Danielou, the reality of Christ through anamnesis exists in three modes: (1) it is the same sacrifice that existed in a precise moment in time, (2) it is now eternally present in heaven, and (3) it "subsists" under the sacramental signs that appear before us. In this manner, Christ's sacrifice as sacrament is made available to all in all times and in all places.[27]

Danielou's thinking regarding the eucharistic anamnesis is echoed by Robert Webber, who speaks of Christ's sacrifice becoming operative once and for all in the present "to the believer who by faith receives Christ under the signs of bread and wine."[28] Similarly, Gregory Dix, in speaking of the Eucharist as anamnesis, notes that the word *anamnēsis* means "a 're-calling' or 're-presenting' of a thing in such a way that it is not so much regarded as being 'absent,' as itself presently operative by its effects." For Dix, anamnesis is an action that Christ has taken, and the consequence is what Jesus meant it to be—his true body and blood. Christ's self-sacrificial action, which for most of the early church constitutes the sacrament, is opposed to the "sacrifice is dependent on the sacrament" approach that many Western churches have adopted.[29] The sacrifice of Christ is stressed as a primary action, that is, the reality the sacrament depends on.

J. D. Crichton, following Dix's thinking, agrees that anamnesis remembers more than just a past event but "recalls into the present the reality of a past event." Crichton's thinking concerning anamnesis is inclusive of the power of the Holy Spirit, which comes by way of Christ's ascension. Christ's ascension is mentioned in the anamnesis and acts "as the bridge between the paschal mystery of Christ and the giving of the Holy Spirit."[30] Simon Chan also sees the work of the Holy Spirit in

---

[26]John Chrysostom, *Homilies on the Epistle to the Hebrews*, ed. Philip Schaff, NPNF First Series (Peabody, MA: Hendrickson Publishers, 1994), XVII.6.

[27]Jean Danielou, SJ, *The Bible and the Liturgy* (Notre Dame, IN: University of Notre Dame Press, 2002), 137-38.

[28]Robert E. Webber, *Worship Old and New* (Grand Rapids, MI: Zondervan, 1994), 181.

[29]Gregory Dom Dix, *The Shape of Liturgy*, new ed. (New York: Bloomsbury, 2005), 245.

[30]J. D. Crichton, "A Theology of Worship," in *The Study of Liturgy*, ed. Cheslyn Jones et al. (New York: Oxford University Press, 1978), 17.

connection to anamnesis. For Chan, within the eucharistic liturgy the Spirit keeps in tension a dual movement of actualizing the past (anamnesis) and anticipating the future (prolepsis) through the epiclesis (invocation of the Holy Spirit).[31]

While the concept of anamnesis has been restricted in Christianity to what occurs within the eucharistic liturgy by the power of the Holy Spirit, its roots are Platonic and can be of help in developing an understanding of the ecumenism of the Spirit being experienced by pentecostals recovering the Great Tradition. How can we view an ecumenism of the Spirit as anamnesis, and to what extent can the prayer of Jesus for unity found in John 17 be considered an anamnesis prayer?

For Plato, learning and inquiry are nothing but a recollection by an immortal soul that has been reborn many times through reincarnation and is able to recall and remember natural information.[32] To prove this point Plato depicts a slave boy who works in Meno's house as a character in dialogue with Socrates. Within the dialogue Socrates questions the slave boy about geometry, even though the boy has never been taught geometry. The boy, through Socrates' questioning, is able to answer the complicated problems presented by using nothing else but the "figures inscribed in the sand at his feet."[33] How can this be explained, Plato asks? The boy's soul must have "had some recollection of a truth seen before he entered human form, a truth locked and forgotten in the recesses of personal memory." R. E. Allen concludes that Plato's theory of anamnesis "is a theory of inference, and it rests on the intentional relations which Forms bear to one another."[34]

What comparisons can be made between the Christian understanding and practice of anamnesis and Plato's theory? For Plato, the soul is an immortal reality that through reincarnated previous existences collects knowledge and therefore has truth before entering a body. Christianity, and

---

[31] Simon Chan, *Liturgical Theology: The Church as Worshiping Community* (Downers Grove, IL: IVP Academic, 2006), 37.

[32] See R. E. Allen, "Anamnesis in Plato's 'Meno and Phadeo,'" *Review of Metaphysics* 13, no. 1 (September 1959): 165; Plato, *Meno* 81b-c.; see also *Symposium* 204a; *Euthydemus* 275c ff; Dominic Scott, *Plato's Meno*, Cambridge Studies in the Dialogues of Plato (Cambridge: Cambridge University Press, 2006).

[33] Allen, "Anamnesis in Plato's 'Meno and Phaedo,'" 166.

[34] Allen, "Anamnesis in Plato's 'Meno and Phaedo,'" 166-67.

for the most part Judaism, does not believe in the concept of reincarnation but rather in the doctrine of the resurrection (Acts 17:32; 1 Cor 15:13-18). This truth is also part of our liturgical worship. As Christians we recite the Nicene Creed, which states, "We look for the resurrection of the dead, and the life of the world to come. Amen." Interestingly, as Christians we do believe in a spiritual rebirth (Jn 3:3-6; 1 Pet 1:23; Titus 3:5), whether through baptism (Catholic, Orthodox) or confession of faith (Protestant).

In regard to the immortality of the soul, Christianity answers in the positive and believes, as the Westminster Confession reminds us, that

> the bodies of men, after death, return to dust, and see corruption; but their souls which neither die nor sleep, having an immortal subsistence, immediately return to God who gave them. The souls of the righteous, being then made perfect in holiness, are received into the highest heavens, where they behold the face of God in light and glory, waiting for the full redemption of their bodies. Westminster Confession of Faith, chapter 32.[35]

The Westminster Confession echoes a classical Christian point regarding the soul made plainly but eloquently in Gregory of Nyssa's *Dialogue on the Soul and the Resurrection* (which resembles to some extent Plato's treatment of the immortal soul in *Meno* and *Phaedo*). The Westminster Confession also echoes the apostle Paul's statement, "We are confident, yes, well pleased rather to be absent from the body and to be present with Lord" (2 Cor 5:8). So, yes, Christianity believes that the soul is immortal, but only inasmuch as the term *immortality* is qualified to mean "that the living soul created in the image of God does not die with physical death and awaits the resurrection for its new form of embodiment."[36]

As stated above, for Plato, the immortal soul collects knowledge and brings that knowledge with it through a process of reincarnation, recalling natural information once it is in human form through memory (anamnesis). Christianity professes to believe in an immortal soul inasmuch it as it is made in the image of God; however, it does not believe in reincarnation but believes in an eschatological resurrection inclusive of the body

---

[35]Westminster Confession of Faith, chapter 32.
[36]Thomas C. Oden, *Classic Christianity: A Systematic Theology* (New York: HarperOne, 1992), 781.

and a spiritual rebirth. So far, it seems as though there is a major disconnect until we consider the following: If we replaced the language of reincarnation with the language of Christian rebirth, how would that terminology fit into the equation? And if we considered the language of rebirth instead of reincarnation, would we then not have to consider the person of the Holy Spirit (rebirth of water and Spirit, Jn 3:5)?

Consider in depth what Plato believes about the soul: she is immortal and has been born many times, she has beheld all things in this world and the next, and there is nothing she has not learnt, so it is not surprising that she can remember what she once knew about virtue and other things.[37] The soul, then, has at least three distinctives: (1) it is feminine; (2) it has beheld, learned, and knows all things; and (3) it can remember and recall the information gathered from this world and the next. Sound familiar? If not, allow me to jog your memory.

In the Hebrew, the word for Spirit is *ruakh*, and it is almost always feminine. In fact, the earliest Christians spoke of the Holy Spirit using feminine characteristics and metaphors. One of the most used feminine metaphors for the Holy Spirit in the early church was that of mother. Melito of Sardis, for example, speaks of the Holy Spirit as "mother" within a baptismal liturgy in the second century.[38] Origen likewise in the third century speaks of the Holy Spirit as "mother" within the context of her relationship with Christ in a preexisting manner.[39] And the writer of the Pseudo-Macarian Homilies, in referring to the darkness that comes over a sinful humanity, speaks of the Holy Spirit as a "kind mother, the grace of the Holy Spirit," which cannot be seen by sinful humanity.[40]

Just as for Plato the soul has beheld, learned, and knows all things, the biblical writers attribute the same to the Holy Spirit. Consider, for example, Paul's discussion of the Holy Spirit with the Corinthians:

---

[37]Plato, *Meno* trans. B. Jowett, Third Oxford Edition (Boston, MA: Actonian Press), Kindle edition, 81.

[38]Melito of Sardis, *On Pascha* fragment 17.

[39]Origen, *Commentary on the Gospel According to John*, trans. Ronald E. Heine, Fathers of the Church 89 (Washington, DC: Catholic University of America Press, 1993), 2, 12.

[40]Pseudo-Macarius, Homily 28.4, in *Pseudo-Macarius: The Fifty Spiritual Homilies and the Great Letter*, ed. and trans. George A. Maloney, Classics of Western Spirituality (Mahwah, NJ: Paulist, 1992), 185.

But as it is written:

> "Eye has not seen, nor ear heard,
> Nor have entered into the heart of man
> The things which God has prepared for those who love Him."

But God has revealed them to us through His Spirit. For the Spirit searches all things, yes, the deep things of God. For what man knows the things of a man except the spirit of the man which is in him? Even so no one knows the things of God except the Spirit of God. Now we have received, not the spirit of the world, but the Spirit who is from God, that we might know the things that have been freely given to us by God.

These things we also speak, not in words which man's wisdom teaches but which the Holy Spirit teaches, comparing spiritual things with spiritual. (1 Cor 2:9-13)

Also up for consideration is the admonishment given to believers in 1 John 2 against being deceived by antichrists: "But you have an anointing from the Holy One, and you know all things. I have not written to you because you do not know the truth, but because you know it, and that no lie is of the truth" (1 Jn 2:20-21). Here John describes the consequence of "knowing all things," with the cause being "anointed by the Holy One," a phrase regularly assumed to be connected with the action of the Holy Spirit.

For Plato, the soul recalls or remembers all things. On this topic one needs to look no further than Jesus' words to his disciples concerning his resurrection, ascension, and the work of the Holy Spirit in John: "These things I have spoken to you while being present with you. But the Helper, the Holy Spirit, whom the Father will send in My name, He will teach you all things, and bring to your remembrance all things that I said to you" (Jn 14:25-26). Further,

> I still have many things to say to you, but you cannot bear them now. However, when He, the Spirit of truth, has come, He will guide you into all truth; for He will not speak on His own authority, but whatever He hears He will speak; and He will tell you things to come. He will glorify Me, for He will take of what is Mine and declare it to you. All things that the Father has are Mine. Therefore, I said that He will take of Mine and declare it to you. (Jn 16:12-15)

These texts reveal not only that the Holy Spirit is both the teacher and reminder of all things but that he will also speak of things to come, a distinctive Plato makes concerning the soul and its ability to recall information from the next world.

Thus we can say that, regarding anamnesis, the soul in Plato's understanding resembles the Holy Spirit's person and role in Scripture. The Spirit, who knows all things, recalls all things, and brings believers to all truth, accomplishes such a reality through a process of an ecclesial, historical, and experiential anamnesis. For adherents of a paleo-orthodox movement in general and a Pentecostal orthodoxy in particular, it is the Spirit himself who not only places a yearning for the spirituality of the Great Tradition in our hearts but through an experiential anamnesis also oversees our trip into the past, introducing us to the patristic writings and Christian liturgies of both the East (Orthodox) and West (Roman Catholic).

In reading the Fathers and Mothers of the church, we become one with them and in essence with the whole church. Their writings do not necessarily make us as pentecostals want to become Roman Catholic, Orthodox, or Anglican (although some might sense that noble call). We do not read about the lives or work of the Fathers and Mothers through a denominational lens but as belonging to the same one, holy, catholic, and apostolic church we belong to.

The same goes for our adoption of historical worship. Not only are we comfortable with the various liturgies encompassed within the Great Tradition (either Eastern or Western), but we share in the same with the "great cloud of witnesses," the church triumphant. In particular, our eucharistic celebrations, through anamnesis in an ecumenism of the Spirit, are had with Athanasius, Irenaeus, Cyprian, and John of Damascus, even though we are technically not allowed to share in the Eucharist with the canonical churches who claim them.

PENTECOSTAL ORTHODOXY AND DIALOGUE WITH ROMAN CATHOLICISM AND EASTERN ORTHODOXY

Now that I have examined how a Pentecostal orthodoxy as a development of an ecumenism of the Spirit recovers the Great Tradition through anamnesis, the last section of this chapter asks, What are some contributions a Pentecostal orthodoxy can make to Pentecostal–Roman Catholic /Orthodox dialogues? The majority, if not all, of historical ecumenical dialogues involving pentecostalism have taken place with classical Pentecostal denominational leaders. Very rarely has nondenominational neo-pentecostalism been invited to engage in ecumenical conversations with other Christian traditions—which, given what we have already learned concerning a Pentecostal orthodoxy, we must now look to remedy. I will consider a couple of areas for each of the dialogues, showing how a Pentecostal orthodox perspective would differ from a classical Pentecostal perspective of the same.[41]

International Catholic-Pentecostal dialogue. According to the Pontifical Council for Promoting Christian Unity, there have been several published dialogues with Pentecostals from 1972–2015.[42] To my knowledge this is one of the longest-running official ecumenical dialogues. Worthy of mention is the outstanding foundational work of David du Plessis (1905–1987) and the excellent developmental work of Cecil M. Robeck Jr. Key to comprehending the dialogues themselves is understanding the effects of the Vatican II document on Christian unity *Unitatis redintegratio*.

According to *Unitatis redintegratio*, the children of the Protestant Reformation communities "are in communion with the Catholic Church even though this communion is imperfect."[43] From a biblical perspective, this concept of imperfect unity is confusing, for "every good and perfect gift is from above, coming down from the Father of lights" (Jas 1:17). How can this unity, which is correctly identified by Cardinal Kasper as a "gift from above, stemming from and growing toward loving communion of the Father, Son and Holy Spirit," be imperfect?[44] Also, if unity is an expression of "the whole depth of God's agape," as Pope John Paul II declares, are

---

[41]Anyone looking to study this matter in depth should consider as a strong starting point the compilation edited by Vondey, *Pentecostalism and Christian Unity: Ecumenical Documents and Critical Assessments*.

[42]"The Pontifical Council for Promoting Christian Unity," Vatican, www.christianunity.va/content/unitacristiani/en/dialoghi/sezione-occidentale/pentecostali/dialogo/documenti-di-dialogo.html.

[43]*Unitatis redintegratio*, n. 3.

[44]Kasper, *Spiritual Ecumenism*, 10.

God's expressions imperfect?[45] Further, if perfect love casts out fear
(1 Jn 4:18), then does imperfect unity not remind love that fear still exists
to a significant extent? Given the various biblical and theological com-
plexities of the term "imperfect unity," a better phrase could have been
used that appropriates the imagery used elsewhere in Vatican II of the
"pilgrim Church" in order to reconceptualize unity among all Christians as
"walking together toward a more perfect unity."

The Decree on the Restoration of Unity goes on to contrast this "imperfect unity" with other Christians with the "perfect unity" that is already
found within the Roman Catholic Church as a whole and that God wills for
all Christians. This perfect unity in the Catholic Church subsists mainly in
apostolic succession, sacraments, magisterial teachings, and papal authority.[46] These areas are some of the same ones Pope John Paul II identifies
as ones "in need of fuller study before true consensus of faith can be
achieved," and also are some of the exact areas discussed within the Catholic-Pentecostal dialogues from 1975–2015.[47] In more detail, these areas are

> 1) The relationship between Sacred Scripture, as the highest authority in
> matters of faith, and Sacred Tradition, as indispensable to the interpretation
> of the Word of God; 2) the Eucharist, as the Sacrament of the Body and
> Blood of Christ, an offering of praise to the Father, the sacrificial memorial
> and Real presence of Christ and the sanctifying outpouring of the Holy
> Spirit; 3) Ordination as a Sacrament, to the threefold ministry of the epis-
> copate, presbyterate and diaconate; 4) the Magisterium of the Church, en-
> trusted to the Pope and the Bishops in communion with him, understood
> as a responsibility and authority exercised in the name of Christ for teaching
> and safeguarding the faith; 5) the Virgin Mary, as Mother of God and Icon
> of the Church, the spiritual Mother who intercedes for Christ's disciples
> and for all humanity.[48]

If an adherent of a Pentecostal orthodoxy had been present in the Catholic-
Pentecostal dialogues, how would they have answered the Catholic Church

---

[45]John Paul II, *Ut unum sint of the Holy Father John Paul II on Commitment to Ecumenism* (Ottawa:
Canadian Conference of Catholic Bishops, 1995), 9.

[46]See *Unitatis redintegratio*, nn. 3-4; *Lumen Gentium*, nn. 8, 22.

[47]John Paul II, *Ut unum sint*, 79.

[48]John Paul II, *Ut unum sint*, 88-89.

in regard to the areas mentioned above? First, as we saw in chapter two, pentecostals are in the process of recovering the riches of a sacramental theology in regard to the Eucharist, in particular the Eucharist as the real body and blood of Christ. There are still some areas where both traditions disagree, of course—such as the conveying of grace in the Eucharist as being distinct from the Word of God, and issues of perceived "mechanical" and "magical" perceptions.[49] But for the most part on the Pentecostal side, as Chris Green's work shows, there has been and continues to be advancement in understanding concerning the subject. A Pentecostal orthodox perspective regarding the Eucharist would have revealed that we too believe in the real body and blood of Christ celebrated weekly in a liturgy inclusive of the words of institution (anamnesis) and an epiclesis by either a priest or a bishop. We do not subscribe to the teaching of transubstantiation but believe, as the Orthodox believe, that the elements of bread and wine become for us the body and the blood of our Lord and Savior Jesus Christ under the power of the Holy Spirit as mystery.

Regarding the Virgin Mary, anyone who examines the dialogues will notice that much suspicion has been eased by clarification of the divide between belief and practice on the Catholic side. Pentecostals, however, still do not see the need for any kind of intercessory role for Mary, or for any saint for that matter, especially as relates to the usage of icons.[50] Within a Pentecostal orthodoxy, because we subscribe to the language of veneration as opposed to worship, it is quite easy for us to confront the issue of Mary. There are those within Pentecostal orthodoxy who have included the veneration of Mary and of saints within their liturgical spirituality, but for the most part we consider these beliefs and actions to be part of the hierarchy of truths we can defend but really do not ever practice.

Concerning iconography, it would shock many to know how many pentecostals exhibit icons in their houses or offices. Pentecostal orthodox

---

[49] *Perspectives on Koinonia: Report from the Third Quinquennium of the Dialogue Between the Pontifical Council for Promoting Christian Unity of the Roman Catholic Church and Some Classical Pentecostal Churches and Leaders (1985–1989)*, 1989, 84-86, www.christianunity.va/content/unitacristiani/en/dialoghi/sezione-occidentale/pentecostali/dialogo/documenti-di-dialogo/testo-in-inglese1.html.

[50] *Final Report of the Dialogue between the Secretariat for Promoting Christian Unity of the Roman Catholic Church and Some Classical Pentecostals (1977–1982)*, 66.

adherents are also quite comfortable with the use of icons, siding with John of Damascus in the iconoclasm controversy at the Second Council of Nicaea in 787. John of Damascus, in contrasting the command in Exodus 33:20 and Deuteronomy 4:15 with Paul's statement in 2 Corinthians 3:18, notes the importance of unseen form in the Old Testament connected to image making and Paul's language of "unveiled" faces beholding the glory of God. In earlier times the glory of God could not be seen, but now it is made available in Christ Jesus. John of Damascus concludes: "When he who is bodiless and without form, immeasurable in the boundlessness of his own nature, existing in the form of God, empties himself and takes the form of a servant in substance and in stature and is found in a body of flesh, then you may draw his image and show it to anyone willing to gaze upon it."[51]

Regarding ministry and ordination, while Catholics see bishop, priest, and deacon as ecclesial offices connected to apostolic succession for the "orderly transmission of ministry through history," Pentecostals generally see ministry and ordination through the "recognition of gifts already imparted," but in general cannot agree among themselves how the church should best be ordered.[52] Adherents of a Pentecostal orthodoxy hold to the historical view of the East and the West concerning ordination as a sacrament to the threefold ministry of bishop, priest, and deacon. We believe not in mere functional gifts empowered by the Spirit but in being *in persona Christi* when it comes to the celebration of the sacraments. One of the main differences, however, is that we remain egalitarian in regard to gender, discovering within both Scripture and tradition evidence for the ordination of women.

Concerning the place of sacred tradition, sacred Scripture, and the role of the magisterium of the church, in the final report of 1972–1976 both traditions agreed, "The church is always subject to sacred Scriptures," even though there was "considerable disagreement as to the role of tradition in interpretation of Scripture." In the final report of 1977–1982 the subject

---

[51]John of Damascus, *On the Divine Images*, trans. Andrew Louth, Popular Patristic Series (New York: St. Vladimir's Seminary Press, 2003), 1.8.
[52]Final Report of the Dialogue, 86, 89; "Perspectives on Koinonia," 84.

was considered further as Catholics conveyed their belief in an authoritative living tradition handed down through the centuries, "experienced by the whole church, guided by church leaders, operative in all aspects of Christian life. This tradition is not a source of revelation separate from Scripture, but Scripture responded to and actualized in the living tradition of the church." Pentecostals responded by disagreeing with Catholics concerning the authority of tradition, maintaining that there is only one authority (Scripture), not two, and that Scripture "must be read and understood with the illumination of the Holy Spirit." For Pentecostals, "Scripture can only be discerned through the Holy Spirit."[53]

In regard to biblical exegesis, contemporary Catholics accept the historical-critical framework, while Pentecostals conveyed their rejection of the principles of form and redaction criticism as "militating against the plenary inspiration of Scripture."[54] In the case of conflicting interpretations of biblical texts, the Catholic Church looks to the living tradition under the guidance of the Holy Spirit as an authentic source for guidance. The living tradition, for Catholics and Pentecostals, is inclusive of patristic writings as providing "genuine and vital testimonies to the faithfulness of God," even though the value each tradition ascribes to these writings differs.[55]

For Catholics this living tradition is inclusive of the "teaching office of the church," that is, the magisterium. Pentecostals, however, in the case of conflicting biblical texts rely on the guidance of the Holy Spirit.[56] Pentecostals present at the dialogues held that Scripture is "clear in all essential points" and that Christians can interpret Scripture for themselves under the guidance of the Holy Spirit.[57] Historically, this type of approach has led to the multiplicity of denominations, and for the most part pentecostals recovering the Great Tradition reject such an approach to the

---

[53]Final Report of the Dialogue, 28, 19-20.

[54]Final Report of the Dialogue, 22-23.

[55]*On Becoming a Christian: Insights from Scripture and Patristic Writings; Report on the Fifth Phase of the International Dialogue Between Some Classical Pentecostal Churches and Leaders and the Catholic Church (1998–2006)*, 2006, www.christianunity.va/content/unitacristiani/en/dialoghi/sezione-occidentale/pentecostali/dialogo/documenti-di-dialogo/testo-del-documento-in-inglese1.html.

[56]"On Becoming a Christian," 52, 26-27.

[57]"Perspectives on Koinonia," 26.

interpretation of Scripture. Rather, as part of the living tradition, we hold to a historical communitarian approach toward interpreting Scripture, inclusive of Vincent of Lérins's commonitorium as our extracanonical normative interpretive arbiter.[58] Pentecostals recovering the Great Tradition would have wondered how much they differed with Catholics on this matter, seeing as both use a communitarian approach to interpreting Scripture inclusive of an extracanonical normative interpretive arbiter (magisterium and Vincent's commonitorium).

In closing this section, I inevitably come to the concept of papal infallibility, which most Christian traditions reject. For some years now, I and other pentecostals recovering the Great Tradition have been conversing about the matter and have come up with some interesting thoughts that could and should be explored further. Without accepting the actual premise, and putting aside its imperialistic undertones, could papal infallibility itself be reconsidered through a prophetic lens that mirrors what occurs in a pentecostal service when a known prophetic person speaks in the Spirit? I have been in services where, when a prophet speaks under the power of the Holy Spirit, those in the audience hearing the prophecy not only accept the word given but believe it as being from God himself. Could the difference be the framework the Catholic Church has constructed around the matter? If the framework were that when the pope speaks *ex cathedra* he does so prophetically under the power of the Spirit as the first among equals, would it not in some way resemble what occurs within most pentecostal services? Seeing as though this infallibility resides in the Catholic Church as well as in the body of bishops in unison with the pope in the magisterium, would a better way to reframe this teaching be to use prophetic imagery that resembles Paul's words concerning prophecy in 1 Corinthians 14:29?[59] ("Let two or three prophets speak, and let the others judge.") What ecumenical implications would this kind of reframing have if Orthodox, Anglican, and, yes, Pentecostal bishops were consulted and included in this type of papal declaration?

---

[58]See John C. Peckham, *Canonical Theology: The Biblical Canon, Sola Scriptura, and the Theological Method* (Grand Rapids, MI: Eerdmans, 2016), 73-139.
[59]Catechism of the Catholic Church, www.vatican.va/archive/ENG0015/_INDEX.HTM.

What would happen if Catholics knew that there were pentecostals who were devoted to the practice of and belief in sacramentality (weekly Eucharist), apostolic succession, living tradition, and ecclesial authority, but were without official (administrative or bureaucratic) connection to the Roman Catholic Church? Why would the Roman Catholic Church not extend some type of status (such as an apostolate) to such an ecclesial community? What manner of unity could exist between the Roman Catholic Church and an emerging Pentecostal orthodox community that was birthed by an ecumenism of the Spirit as a direct response to the prayer of Jesus and the work of Vatican II?

Orthodox-Pentecostal dialogue. Orthodox-Pentecostal dialogue is more recent than Catholic-Pentecostal dialogue. The two official Orthodox-Pentecostal academic dialogues (2017–2018) recorded were preceded by informal conversations between representatives of the ecumenical patriarch and classic Pentecostals between 2010 and 2012.[60] For the most part, if continued, this dialogue should yield considerable developments, since in recent years research from both traditions reveals that Pentecostals and the Orthodox have much in common. Although there is not much ecumenically to develop yet, I offer a brief word on what the two traditions share in common along with how pentecostals recovering the Great Tradition might contribute to the dialogues.

In his book *Beyond Salvation*, Edmund Rybarczyk provides a brief but comprehensive list of the similarities between classic Pentecostalism and Eastern Orthodoxy. For Rybarczyk both traditions practice an experiential mystical spirituality, hold to an organic ecclesial authoritative structure, emphasize the role of the laity, and allow their clergy to marry. Finally, but most importantly, both traditions see themselves as defenders of pneumatology.[61] In regard to an organic ecclesial structure, most Pentecostal denominations have historically put in place structures that resemble the Orthodox concepts of autocephalous administration, the

---

[60]"Orthodox-Pentecostal Academic Dialogue," *Journal of Pentecostal Theology* 28 (2019): 163-64.

[61]Edmund J. Rybarczyk, *Beyond Salvation: Eastern Orthodoxy and Classical Pentecostalism on Becoming like Christ* (Eugene, OR: Wipf & Stock, 2004), 2-9. On pentecostals practicing an experiential mystical spirituality, see Daniel Castelo's argument in chapter two.

monarchic episcopate, and the principle of canonical territory.[62] Pentecostals recovering the Great Tradition usually adopt an Orthodox autocephalous relational structure, which calls for collegiality and is not
patriarchal. In regard to ecumenism and structure, Rybarczyk's argument
concerning how pentecostalism shares Orthodoxy's decentralized
structure is especially true for the Greek Orthodox Church. According to
Irvin, in the Greek Orthodox Church "the fall of Constantinople in 1453
effectively removed the 'political overtones' of the word *ecumenical*, giving
way for the term to take on a more mystical meaning after 1453."[63] Irvin
further states,

> The unity that accompanied the ecumenical experience came to be seen
> as being more dependent on the inner working of the Holy Spirit in the
> life of the church than in the external exercise of political authority. Unity
> through love and obedience came to be closely associated with the formal
> unity of doctrine and practice, which remains in Orthodox theology
> grounded on the unity of the ancient ecumenical councils and adherence
> to the Nicene Creed.[64]

While the Roman Catholic Church continues to hold in tension the imperial and religious connotation of the word *ecumenical*, pentecostals recovering the Great Tradition hold to a mystical understanding of
ecumenism similar to that of the Greek Orthodox Church post-1453.

Although the Orthodox Church believes itself to be *the* one, holy,
catholic, and apostolic church, there are those within the church who, according to Kallistos Ware, acknowledge that some outside the Orthodox
Church can be considered as belonging to the church.[65] According to Ware,
this moderate group believes,

> There is only one Church, but there are many different ways of being related
> to this one Church, and many different ways of being separated from it.
> Some non-Orthodox are very close indeed to Orthodoxy, others less so;

---

[62]Hilarion Alfeyev, *Orthodox Christianity*, vol. 1, *The History and Canonical Structure of the Orthodox Church* (Yonkers, NY: St. Vladimir's Seminary Press, 2019), 325-38.
[63]Irvin, "Specters of a New Ecumenism," 7-8.
[64]Irvin, "Specters of a New Ecumenism," 7-8.
[65]Kallistos Timothy Ware, *The Orthodox Church*, 3rd ed. (London: Penguin Books, 2015), 308.

some are friendly to the Orthodox Church, others indifferent or hostile. By God's grace the Orthodox Church possesses the fullness of truth (so its members are bound to believe), but there are other Christian communions which possess to a greater or lesser degree a genuine measure of Orthodoxy. All these facts must be taken into account: one cannot simply say that all non-Orthodox are outside the Church, and leave it at that; one cannot treat other Christians as if they stood on the same level as unbelievers.[66]

That the Orthodox Church believes itself to be the one true church is the basis for its desire for all Christians to be reconciled to Orthodoxy. However, the Orthodox Church does not believe in intercommunion but rather a full communion that is predicated on unity in matters of faith, which precedes communion in the sacraments.

For Rybarczyk, Pentecostals and Orthodox share similarities relating to mystical spirituality and organizational structure, but it must also be noted that the Orthodox and Pentecostals share similar criticisms of the Roman Catholic Church. Ware mentions the *filioque*, papal authority, purgatory, and the immaculate conception, all of which pentecostalism also criticizes.

For the most part, pentecostals recovering the Great Tradition have done so using mainly a Western lens (Catholic or Anglican). With the exception of a few communities, theology, liturgical and sacramental spirituality, prayer books, and even dress reflect a more Western way of recovery. However, there continues to be considerable interest in recovering the Great Tradition from an Eastern expression among pentecostals. The liturgy of John Chrysostom and that of Basil as practiced in the Orthodox Church have greatly interested pentecostals recovering ancient spirituality due to their mystical connotations. Also, following the lead of Pentecostal scholars such as Steven Land, Daniela Augustine, and Dale Coulter, pentecostals recovering the Great Tradition are beginning to take interest in Eastern fathers such as Macarius, Symeon, Palamas, and John Climacus, just to mention a few.

Conclusion. Now that I have attempted to set Pentecostal orthodoxy within the broader ecumenical discussion, we can ask, What would be the

---

[66]Ware, *Orthodox Church*, 308-9.

clear goals for ecumenical discussions on the part of adherents of Pentecostal orthodoxy with other Christian traditions? What type of recognition or participation could be considered, and in what ways could other Christian traditions (Catholic, Orthodox, Anglican) reflect on the branch of pentecostalism that recovers the historic Great Tradition?

For starters, a Pentecostal orthodox–Anglican discussion could yield tremendous benefits for both traditions. First, as already noted above, as pentecostals and charismatics began their recovery of the Great Tradition, most did so through an Anglican or Methodist framework (Webber and Oden). In regard to liturgy, I use a revised and contextualized version of the eucharistic liturgy Rite I in the 1979 Book of Common Prayer and personally know at least twenty other pentecostal ministers who use the same. Theologically, pentecostals recovering the great tradition believe in about 98 percent of what Anglicans believe in and know a majority of Anglican history, due to Pentecostalism's closeness to Methodism. Anglicans, on the other hand, often have a strong sense of the charismatic movement. Some Anglicans even confess that they speak and pray in tongues and believe in spiritual warfare and in the baptism of the Holy Spirit. Could Anglicans be in full communion with pentecostals recovering the Great Tradition? After a survey of their work, liturgy, and apostolic succession, could Anglicanism recognize their orders, ordain some *sub conditione* (under some type of condition), or pass on lines of succession in order to be in full communion?

A Pentecostal orthodox–Orthodox dialogue would not necessarily lend itself to full communion but would give both traditions cause for reflection as they came to know about each other. First, given that a Pentecostal orthodoxy to a large extent can be situated within the mystical and monastic movements of the church, what similarities between Greek, African, and even Syrian Christian monastic mysticism and Pentecostal orthodoxy could be examined? Could the sense of cenobitic asceticism and holiness inherent in pentecostalism as a whole, combined with the recovery of the Great Tradition, give cause for the Orthodox to consider such common spiritual similarities with monasticism? Furthermore, since Syrian Orthodoxy is highly pnuematological, what commonalities could be found from a Pentecostal orthodox rereading of the Odes of

Solomon, the Acts of Thomas, the writings of Aphrahat, or the theology of Saint Ephrem?

In the Orthodox tradition, most recognize the existence of two forms of apostolic succession within the life of the church, as His Eminence Kallistos Ware points out: "First there is the visible succession of the hierarchy, the unbroken series of bishops in different cities. . . . Alongside this, largely hidden, existing on a 'charismatic' rather than an official level, there is secondly the apostolic succession of the spiritual fathers and mothers in each generation of the Church."[67] Could this type of succession, referred to by Saint Symeon the New Theologian and others as "the golden chain," be considered to be had by pentecostals recovering the Great Tradition?

Finally, there exists today mostly in the Antiochian Orthodox tradition a segment of Orthodoxy known as "Western Rite" Orthodoxy. These groups have removed the *filioque* from the proclamation of the Nicene Creed and maintain a Western liturgy, usually a Gallican rite or an Anglican rite inclusive of an epiclesis.[68] Given, that most penecostals recovering the Great Tradition use some type of Western Anglican rite in their liturgy, could a Pentecostal orthodoxy be considered as Western Rite if it was looking to become Orthodox?

Last, there already exists an almost fifty-year history of a rich and fruitful international Roman Catholic–Pentecostal dialogue. Cecil Robeck, a leading voice and influence in the dialogue, notes that for Pentecostals little theological competence is expected for a person to become a believer, and yet when it comes to recognizing Roman Catholics as Christian believers, complex expectations and requirements are established. In return, according to Robeck, "Catholics have refused to recognize the genuine Christian character of Pentecostals and their denominations."[69] This kind of religious animosity has led to strained working relationships, especially

---

[67]Kallistos Ware, "The Sacrament of Baptism and the Ascetic Life in the Teaching of Mark the Monk," in *Studia Patristica* 10 (Berlin, 1970), 299.

[68]Those looking for more information on this matter would benefit from Michael Keiser's *Children of the Promise: An Introduction to Western Rite Orthodoxy* (Bloomington, IN: AuthorHouse Publishers, 2004).

[69]Cecil M. Robeck, "Lessons from the International Catholic-Pentecostal Dialogue," in *Pentecostalism and Christian Unity: Ecumenical Documents and Critical Assessments* (Eugene, OR: Pickwick, 2010), 85.

in places such as Latin America. Yet, with the exception of a few doctrinal items (purgatory, transubstantiation, and so on) that most Pentecostal orthodox adherents I know would not buy into, what new and fresh perspectives and frameworks would a Catholic-Pentecostal dialogue inclusive of pentecostals who believe 98 percent of what Roman Catholics do bring about? For example, is there a way for pentecostals recovering the Great Tradition to better reflect on the matter of papal infallibility through the lens of the authority and respect granted to a prophet during divine ecstatic speech in a Pentecostal service? Could Roman Catholics include pentecostals recovering the Great Tradition in the Catholic Fraternity of Charismatic Covenant Communities and Fellowships in even more direct ways? Could such a relationship between Catholics and Pentecostals recovering the Great Tradition be considered a missionary apostolate of sorts? Is there a way to see such a relationship as similar to the Catholic Fraternity of Charismatic Covenant Communities and Fellowships, only without being in full communion with the successor of Peter (especially when most pentecostals recovering the Great Tradition historically understand him hierarchically to be the first among equals)?

These questions should give cause for consideration no matter how absurd they may seem. On all fronts and in all dialogues with all traditions, the question of the eucharistic liturgy will always be the elephant in the room. How much of the liturgy would Catholics, Anglicans, and Orthodox allow Pentecostal orthodox adherents to participate in? Would adherents of a Pentecostal orthodoxy reciprocate? How much would they allow others from other traditions to participate in our liturgical services?

CONCLUSION

"HOW MUCH FURTHER MUST WE STILL TRAVEL until that blessed day when full unity in faith will be attained and we can celebrate together in peace the Holy Eucharist of the Lord?"[1] The question asked by Pope John Paul II reveals the ever-increasing ecclesial tension between the unity we have and the unity we seek. Do we have an "imperfect unity"? Alternatively, in light of the Spirit's work and action, can we rethink that concept and look toward adopting an attitude of walking together, continuing to walk in the light of the unity that already exists? If the biblical story of the two disciples on the Emmaus Road teaches us anything about walking together, it is that every journey ends in breaking bread together. Yet, although the prayer of Jesus within the framework of a conciliar, Spirit-led activity seems to have found a springboard toward visible unity in Vatican II, the question must be asked, What more is required of us?

After considering a Pentecostal orthodoxy as a post–Vatican II ecclesiological development, and after acknowledging an ecumenism of the Spirit at work within the church, one must consider whether the extra travel we Christians now do is an unnecessary, independent journey, the end of which embodies the fractured sacred meal in 1 Corinthians 11. Cardinal Edward Cassidy says, "In the search for that full and visible communion,

---

[1]John Paul II, *Ut unum sint of the Holy Father John Paul II on Commitment to Ecumenism* (Ottawa: Canadian Conference of Catholic Bishops, 1995), 77.

Christians may be sure that God will not let them down. But can we be sure that the Christians themselves will not let God down?"[2] Can we move away from a solely professional ecumenism, considering, as Harold Hunter does, "If Roman Catholics are not the only members of the church catholic, if the Greek Orthodox are not the only orthodox, are professional ecumenists the only ecumenists?"[3]

As we conclude our conversation, we must be cognizant of the *what* and *where* in regard to walking toward this new ecumenical horizon together. What answers do we have for an eschatological manifestation of the kingdom of God as a right-now-but-not-yet, mystical, and pragmatic reality concerning visible unity? Are we willing to manifest our unity and communion through a historical ecclesiological modality that incorporates its manifestation as the ultimate *eschata* (teaching of the last things) concerning the church of Jesus Christ?[4] Is this the time when we awaken from our deep sleep in order to acquiesce to the heeding of the Spirit, who "teaches people to interpret carefully the 'signs of the times'"?[5] Or will we continue to be plagued by a Constantinian memory of ecumenism, in which specters haunt us by continuing to politicize our unity, seeking unity with a top-down-only, heads-of-state mentality, all the while oblivious to the moving of the Spirit in lesser-known charismatic ecclesial communities?

We must again take care that we do not take Jesus' prayer for unity and make it out to become an ontological institutional yearning that continues to promote the one true petition for unity while suspiciously keeping at arm's length the one true action of unity. Winston Churchill said, "To improve is to change; to be perfect is to have changed often."[6] Change, or

---

[2] Edward Idris Cardinal Cassidy, *Ecumenism and Interreligious Dialogue: Unitatis Redintegratio, Nostra Aetate*, Rediscovering Vatican II (New York: Paulist, 2005), 110.

[3] Harold D. Hunter, "Global Pentecostalism and Ecumenism: Two Movements of the Holy Spirit?," in *Pentecostalism and Christian Unity: Ecumenical Documents and Critical Assessments* (Eugene, OR: Pickwick, 2010), 25.

[4] John D. Zizioulas, *Being as Communion: Studies in Personhood and the Church* (New York: St. Vladimir's Seminary Press, 1985), 20.

[5] John Paul II, *Ut unum sint*, 3.

[6] *Winston Churchill: His Complete Speeches, 1897-1963*, ed. Robert Rhodes James, vol. 4, *1922-1928* (New York: Chelsea Publishers, 1974), 3706.

renewal, within the ecumenical movement must always and unquestionably be fostered by the Spirit's leading.

As we walk together toward a more perfect unity, an emphasis on spiritual ecumenism, while commendable, must be balanced with a recognition of an ecumenism of the Spirit. This brings us to reconsider the prayer-without-intentional-action perspective, recalling that "we can do more than pray, after we have prayed, but we cannot do more than pray, until we have prayed."[7] We are once again faced with the reality that it is an ecumenism of the Spirit that sovereignly merges us, bidding us to walk together, with real ramifications in the world through mutual recognition.

The prayer of Jesus reveals his yearning for unity in his church, but it is the Spirit's leading and action that fulfills that prayer. An ecumenism of the Spirit brings us together in love, not only of neighbor and of God but of his one, holy, catholic, and apostolic church. This work is not only the work of doctrinal or political correctness among clerics or theologians but the work of the Holy Spirit. The Spirit, through leaders, lay leaders, and members alike, continues to ontologically guide the church, the whole church, to its predetermined end through love, preparing the bride for the Groom to come. In this love and because of it, we reach out toward each other, simultaneously reaching up toward the heavens, walking together toward a more perfect unity, allowing the light of Christ to continue to pierce the fading darkness.

---

[7] *The Works of John Bunyan*, ed. George Offor, rev. ed. (Edinburgh: Banner of Truth Publishers, 1992), 1:65.

INDEX